The Insurance Industry in Canada

THE ECONOMICS
OF THE SERVICE SECTOR
IN CANADA

Series Editors:
Herbert G. Grubel
Michael A. Walker

The Insurance Industry in Canada

Jeffrey I. Bernstein and
Randall R. Geehan

THE FRASER INSTITUTE

This study is part of a general programme of research into the services sector made possible by a contribution from the Department of Regional Industrial Expansion, Government of Canada.

Canadian Cataloguing in Publication Data

Bernstein, Jeffrey Ian, 1950-
The insurance industry in Canada
(The Economics of the service sector in Canada,
ISSN 0835-4227)
Bibliography: p.
ISBN 0-88975-111-0
1. Insurance - Canada. I. Geehan, Randall.
II. Fraser Institute (Vancouver, B.C.). III. Title.
IV. Series.
HG8550.B47 1988 338.4'7368971 C88-091323-1

Printed in Singapore.

To

Abraham and Minnie Bernstein

and

Oswald and Grace Geehan

Contents

CHAPTER 4
PRODUCTION AND COST OF INSURANCE SERVICES / 35

CHAPTER 5
INSURANCE COMPANIES AS FINANCIAL INTERMEDIARIES / 57

CHAPTER 6
INNOVATION AND INFORMATION / 73

Tables and Figures

Tables

Figures

Figures

Preface and Summary

The purchase of insurance services is pervasive in the contemporary Canadian economy. Homes are insured, cars are insured, lives are insured, health care is insured, and employment is insured. Indeed, insurance services represent 0.76 percent of total services and 0.46 percent of the gross domestic product of the Canadian economy.

The first purpose of this monograph is to analyze the structure of the insurance industry, the role of insurers as financial intermediaries, the demand for insurance, and the production of insurance services. The second purpose is to draw out the relevant policy conclusions from the analysis. The focus of government policy for the insurance industry has centered on competition, regulation and taxation.

The insurance industry includes life (individual and group life and annuities and pension fund management), accident and sickness (health care, dental care, and disability) and property and casualty (vehicles, real property and liability). In terms of premiums, in 1985 the private sector components of the industry were: life insurance 49.1 percent, accident and sickness 8.8 percent and property and casualty 42.1 percent. Over the period 1961-85, insurance firms have experienced average annual (output) growth rates of 4.4 percent which has equaled the rate for the economy as a whole and has surpassed the growth rate of 4.1 percent for manufacturing. However, the components of the industry have grown at substantially different rates. Life insurers have had an average annual growth rate of 5.8 percent, while property and casualty insurers have only grown by 2.8 percent annually.

Prices of insurance policies like prices of other commodities have risen over the last two and a half decades. In comparison with the CPI which has grown annually by 8.2 percent between 1971 and 1985, the prices of tenant and homeowner insurance have grown annually by 12.3 percent and 13.1 percent respectively. Although the inflation rates of these two policies has been one and half times faster than the CPI, the price of life insurance policies has grown annually about half as fast as the CPI, while the price for auto insurance policies has increased in line with the CPI.

The Canadian insurance industry is not concentrated in the hands of a few firms. Entry is relatively easy. Indeed, in 1985 the percentage of net premiums written by the largest four firms writing property and casualty policies was 18.1 percent. In the life insurance segment, the degree of concentration was relatively higher but still only 42.7 percent of net premiums were accounted by the four largest companies. In fact in 1985 there were 167 life insurance firms operating in Canada.

Purchasers of insurance policies buy financial protection from insurance firms because these companies have created the facilities to pool risks. Thus, insurance firms actually provide a form of financial intermediation, and indeed engage in a wide variety of other intermediary roles. Relative to total financial assets, the size of life insurance firms' financial assets has been falling over the post World War Two period. In particular, the industry's holdings of mortgage assets has declined since the 1960s, when about 30 percent of all mortgages in Canada were held by the industry, to about 13 percent in recent years. A change in NHA mortgages from a 25 to a 5-year term has been the chief cause of this shift in the mortgage market.

Government tax policy has had significant effects on the demand for life insurance and on the product mix. Policies which have encouraged savings through tax sheltered RRSPs have increased demand for annuities both by individuals who initially register their RRSPs with a life company, and by those who purchase a life annuity upon maturity of an RRSP originally registered with another financial institution.

Apart from changes in product demand caused by tax changes, there has been a pronounced customer shift away from whole life policies and toward term insurance. This shift has resulted in smaller amounts of funds under the control of life companies and has been the single most important factor explaining the secular decline in the relative size of insurance company financial assets.

Direct regulation of the industry has been aimed at influencing the portfolio demand of insurers. Regulation of asset structures has been designed to protect policy holders. However, there is little evidence that this regulation has in practice influenced companies' portfolio decisions.

Households purchase over half of all insurance services. About 5 percent goes to exports and the bulk of the remainder is purchased as intermediate inputs by industry, chiefly finance insurance and real estate.

Both cross-sectional (i.e., across demanders) and time-series analyses show the demand for insurance services to respond to income changes. Indeed, in the cross-section context a 1 percent increase in income causes the demand for insurance to increase by 1.25 percent. The percentage change is somewhat greater over time. The income effect implies, in the absence of insurance price changes relative to the CPI, that the secular growth rate of insurance is higher than the growth rate of income, but also that insurance demand is subject to wider fluctuations over the business cycle compared to income. Income changes affect insurance services, and indeed services in general, relatively more than the demands for non-durables, semi-durables and durable commodities.

Price changes also affect the demand for insurance services. A 1 percent increase in the price of insurance services causes the demand to fall by 1.3 percent. This estimate implies that a policy of increasing prices cause revenues from sales to decline, given that income and other demographic effects are not changing. As for income, price changes affect the demand for all services including insurance relatively more than the demand for other types of commodities.

The production of insurance services does not constitute a natural monopoly. Economies of scale (or specialization) and economies of scope (or diversity) are not pervasive in the industry. Thus the industry is characterized by a large number of firms with significant diversity of sizes. There are no significant entry barriers and prices appear to be equal to average cost so that there is little if any supra-competitive profit. However, there are substantial differences in prices among insurers for similar policies. These price differences may exist because there are significant product quality differences such as differences in claims handling and in part because of the costly acquisition of price information by consumers.

The issue of scale economies is relevant to horizontal merger policy. Horizontal mergers in the presence of scale economies can reduce unit costs and thereby prices and also increase efficiency within the industry. However, there is no strong evidence of scale economies in the industry.

The existence of scope economies plays an important role in the determination of the efficiency consequences of conglomerate mergers. These mergers are relevant to entry deregulation of the four pillars; insurance firms, chartered banks, security dealers and trust companies. The existence of significant economies of scope implies that there could be efficiency gains from mergers across firms in these different markets. Yet, evidence on scope economies is extremely scarce and what evidence there is concludes that economies are rather weak for the insurance industry.

Labour productivity in the life insurance industry grew at an average annual rate of 3.95 percent which exceeded the annual growth rate in manufacturing of 3.08 percent and for the economy as a whole of 2.77 percent. However, labour productivity in the property and casualty industry was virtually stagnant over the 1975 to 1985 decade. In addition, over the time period 1978 to 1985 total factor productivity for the insurance industry, as a whole, grew at a 1.00 percent average annual rate, which compares favorably with estimates for total manufacturing.

Insurance firms have been reactive rather than innovative in designing new products. This stance has contributed to the decline in assets of the industry relative to other financial institutions. However the pace of product innovation has increased over the last decade.

Canadian life insurers have been successful in extending their operation to other countries. Indeed, in 1985 40 percent of global premium income of companies operating in Canada was earned from foreign operations. Relative to the total value of insurance services produced in Canada, exports and imports are in the range of 5 percent to 7 percent, with exports roughly 90 percent of imports. Canada, along with most foreign countries, requires that domestic assets of insurance companies be held against domestic liabilities. The objective of this regulation has been prudential, aimed at ensuring financial health of the industry and financial safety for policyholders. But the regulation is also protectionist and serves to reduce international trade in insurance services.

Acknowledgements

The authors would like to thank the following people for comments which helped improve the study: Mike Walker, Herb Grubel, Erwin Diewert, an anonymous referee and commentators from the Department of Regional Industrial Expansion. Jeffrey Bernstein would also like to thank Len Fitz-Patrick for computer assistance. Randall Geehan would like to thank Gary MacDonald for research assistance.

About the Authors

Jeffrey I. Bernstein is Professor of Economics and Director, Centre for Quantitative Social Sciences at Carleton University in Ottawa, Canada. Born in Montreal in 1950, he received his B.A. (Honours) degree in economics in 1971 from Sir George Williams University (now Concordia). Professor Bernstein received his M.A. in economics from the University of Western Ontario in 1972 and received his Ph.D. in 1975 from Western, where he was a Canada Council Doctoral Fellow.

Professor Bernstein has been associated with the Departments of Economics at the University of Guelph, Concordia University and McGill University. He has also been a member of the Institute of Applied Economic Research, Concordia University; the Centre for the Study of Regulated Industries, McGill University, the National Bureau of Economic Research, Cambridge, U.S.A. and the C.V. Starr Centre for Applied Economic Research, New York University.

Professor Bernstein's research interests have been in the areas of industrial economics, financial economics and applied microeconomics. Specifically his work has related to industrial production and pricing, technological change and research and development, consumer demand and portfolio analysis. He has published in a number of scholarly journals including the *International Economic Review, the Review of Economic Studies, the Canadian Journal of Economics* and the *American Economic Review,* and he has also written a book on *R&D Investment and Taxation in Canada* published by the University of Toronto Press.

Randall R. Geehan is an Associate Professor of Economics at Carleton University in Ottawa, Canada. Born in Calgary, Alberta in 1945, Professor Geehan received his B.A. in 1966 from Queen's University, M.A. degrees in Economics from the University of Calgary in 1969 and Carleton University in 1974, an M.Sc. in Operational Research from the London School of Economics in 1971 and his Ph.D. in 1977 from MIT. Besides teaching economics at Carleton University, he has held several research and managerial positions at Statistics Canada.

Professor Geehan's research interests centre on applied microeconomics. Specifically, his research has focused on financial institutions and national income accounts, output and productivity measurement in the services industries and consumer demand analysis. He has published a number of journal articles in the *Canadian Journal of Economics, the Rand Journal, the Review of Economics and Statistics* and the *International Journal of Industrial Organization.*

Chapter 1

Introduction and Overview

Nearly everyone buys insurance. If you have a mortgage on your house, the mortgage company requires you to buy a homeowner's policy. You cannot obtain a licence plate for your car without insurance. Your employer may pay for part or all of the expense of group life and extended health care or dental care insurance plans. Your pension plan may be managed by a life insurance company. If you contribute to an RRSP, you must collapse it, buy an RRIF or buy an annuity from a life insurance company before age 71.

Despite the ubiquity of insurance, the nature of the product and the industry are little understood by the average person. An insurance policy is a complex financial instrument (a contingent claim, in economic jargon) which pays the policyholder prescribed sums contingent upon the occurrence of certain insured events (i.e., under prescribed states of nature). Policyholders demand insurance to reduce the variability of their wealth or their survivors' wealth. The purpose of this study is to explain the characteristics and importance of the industry in the economy, describe its products and discuss the policy issues affecting the industry.

This monograph contains considerable descriptive material but also a number of original contributions. The cross-section and time series analyses of consumer demand for insurance in chapter 3 have not been presented before, and the measures of real output and productivity in chapter 4 are new.

We give arguments for a number of changes in Statistics Canada's methodologies. In particular, new estimates of real output for life and property/casualty are presented. We advocate a new imputation for the interest forgone on property/casualty policyholders' advances to insurers (chapter 4). The consumer price index currently contains no measure for life insurance services; we propose one in chapter 2.

The scope of this monograph encompasses insurance carriers for the period 1961-85. Both the time period and the industry definition are determined, in part, by data availability. Statistics Canada's input/output tables and Financial Flow Accounts go back to 1961. Insurance carriers belong to one industry in Statistics Canada's system, and independent agents are in another. Most property/casualty insurance is sold through independent agents, while most life insurance is sold by agents Statistics Canada classifies as company employees.

There are two classes of insurance carriers as defined by the products they sell. Life insurance carriers sell life insurance and annuities, manage pension funds and sell health insurance (also called accident and sickness insurance). Property/casualty insurers (also called general insurers or property/liability or fire and casualty insurers) offer a wide range of products from insurance on real estate, autos, airplanes and ships, to credit insurance and insurance against court judgments for liability.

Chapter 2 begins with a description (supported by statistical data) of the world insurance market, the structure of the Canadian industry, its size and growth, employment and wages, and its price performance, including a new measure of price for life insurance services. This material provides a necessary preliminary perspective and foundation for the analyses in following chapters.

Chapter 3 focuses on the demand for insurance, starting with an accounting of the sources of supply and demand by sector (demand by business, government and households, plus exports) and moving to a detailed analysis of household demand. Here we present original work using cross-section and time series data. We found that the demand for insurance responds strongly and positively to changes in income (the effect is higher for life insurance, much lower for property/casualty insurance). As a result, the secular growth is at a higher rate than is the rate for income growth. Demand also responds strongly and negatively to price increases, implying that price increases reduce sales revenues. Demographic variables (age and sex of household head, size of household, geographic location, homeowner versus tenant), which also have a strong influence on demand are analysed in chapter 3 as well. These demand analyses help explain the growth performance of the industry.

Chapter 4 analyses the production technology of the industry and presents new measures of real output and productivity. Our results show quite high growth in labour productivity for life insurance but a flat trend in output per employee in property/casualty. Total factor productivity also shows respectable growth but has fluctuated over the period 1961-85. In addition, this chapter analyses the evidence for and significance of returns to scale (or economies of specialization) and economies of scope (or returns to product diversity) in insurance. Returns to scale help explain industry structure. Little is yet known about the significance of economies of scope in the insurance industry.

Chapter 5 analyses life and property/casualty as financial institutions, with particular attention to the causes of the relative decline of life insurance assets. Changes in product mix and the decline of the industry's mainstay, the whole life policy, provide the main explanation. The significance of the insurance industry in markets for specific financial instruments is also examined. Life insurers ceased to be the major participant in residential mortgage markets during the period covered by our analysis, largely as a result of changes in the characteristics of the mortgage instrument. There is little evidence that regulation plays a significant role in portfolio behaviour.

Chapter 6 briefly surveys several topics of current interest to researchers and policymakers: innovation in products and processes, information asymmetries between insurers and insured, and differentiation by age and sex in setting insurance rates.

The final chapter discusses policy issues and arrives at a number of conclusions drawing on the material developed previously. Productivity performance in the industry is healthy, as are the competitive conditions in the industry (with the exception of the industry monopoly on product distribution). The four firm concentration ratios are low in both life and property/casualty. The prospects for increased foreign trade in insurance are limited by the fact that most countries, including Canada, require domestic assets to be held against the liabilities related to domestic business. Opportunities abroad are largely confined to setting up subsidiaries in foreign countries—opportunities well exploited by Canadian life companies. Future opportunities for growth in the life business are favourable and are encouraged by the characteristics of demand, evidence of recently improved product innovations and good productivity performance.

Chapter 2

Industry Structure

INTRODUCTION

An overview of the structure of the insurance industry in Canada is preceded by a global perspective on industry activity. This chapter also contains data and comparative analysis on industry growth rates, employment, and wages and prices. Comparisons among total economy, total manufacturing, total finance insurance and real estate (FIRE), and insurance industry data are made where relevant.

A GLOBAL PERSPECTIVE ON THE INSURANCE INDUSTRY

The "GNP elasticity of demand" for insurance, i.e., the ratio of the percentage increase in national expenditure on insurance to the percentage increase in gross national product per capita, is greater than one. This is equivalent to the observation that the share of insurance in GNP increases as GNP per capita rises (see Wasow 1986:173). At lower income levels, this elasticity is higher than at higher levels of GNP per capita (Baker 1987:196). The more wealthy countries spend a larger fraction of income on insurance, and they control a larger share of world incomes. The U.S. and other developed countries overwhelmingly dominate the world market (see table 1). Canada ranks fifth among all countries in total life insurance premiums and sixth in non-life; but when measured in proportion to GNP, Canada ranked second only to Japan in 1985 in life insurance (*Canadian Life and Health Insurance Association Facts*, hereinafter referred to as CLHIA *Facts*).

A number of trends have significantly changed the world market since the Second World War. The share of the North American market has fallen from about 75 percent in the early 1950s to 54 percent in 1984. Japan's share has increased from less than 3 percent in 1964 to nearly 15 percent in 1984. British domination of the international market a quarter of a century ago has given way to American, Japanese and European (especially Swiss and Ger-

Table 1

World's Ten Largest Insurance Countries in Terms of Premiums in 1984

Country	GDP/Capita (in US $)	Life (percent)	Non-Life (percent)	Total (percent)	GDP in US $ (in billions)	Percent of World Total
U.S.A.	15,357	43.5	56.6	50.9	3,635	30.5
Japan	10,263	23.9	7.8	14.8	1,232	10.3
West Germany	10,025	6.2	6.8	6.5	613	5.1
Great Britain	7,533	7.2	3.8	5.3	425	3.6
France	8,907	2.7	4.7	3.8	489	4.1
Canada	13,400	3.3	3.1	3.2	336	2.8
Australia	11,720	1.2	2.2	1.8	182	1.5
Italy	6,114	0.5	2.3	1.5	348	2.9
Netherlands	8,533	1.3	1.2	1.2	123	1.0
Switzerland	14,146	1.3	1.0	1.1	91	0.7
Total of Ten Largest Countries		91.1	89.5	90.1	7,474	62.6

Sources: Baker 1987, and table 1, *National Accounts Statistics: Analysis of Main Aggregates, 1983/84*, New York, United Nations, 1986.

man) competitors. In non-life or property/casualty insurance there has been a boom in captive insurance companies which are customer-owned and exclusively serve one or a few parent companies. The captives are often located offshore for tax reasons. As many as 1,000 are located in Bermuda alone. (The phenomenon of captive insurance companies is discussed in chapter 6.) The share of life insurance relative to non-life has fallen in the world market during every post-war decade save the 1980s.

Two phenomena of international trade in insurance services that are worth noting are the growth of international brokerage firms serving the needs of multinational corporations and international re-insurance. Insurance companies can diversify and reduce the risk of their liabilities by reselling shares of policies to other firms. This is re-insurance. Insurance companies both buy and sell risks among themselves, but some firms specialize as re-insurers. In Canada, most life re-insurance is done within Canada's borders, but increasing amounts of property/casualty re-insurance business flow across borders. Some risks, such as insuring airlines against property losses and liability claims from the families of accident victims, are simply too large for one or even a few companies to handle.

Table 2
Components of the Canadian Industry for Insurance Carriers
(1985 premiums in millions of dollars)

Life Insurance		
Federally registered companies	$10,445	79.9%
Provincially registered companies	651	5.0
Accident and sickness (health insurance) branches of life companies	1,982	15.1
Total—Life Insurance	13,078	100.0
Property and Casualty Insurance		
Federally registered companies	$ 7,978	72.2%
Provincially licensed private companies	1,546	14.0
Provincial government insurance corporations	1,522	13.8
Total—Property and Casualty	11,046	100.0

Sources: Federal Superintendent of Insurance Annual Report 1985, and Canadian Life and Health Insurance Facts, 1985.

Notes: Data are for business in Canada only. Canadian life companies earned an additional $5,636 million in life and annuity premium income abroad in 1985, and Canadian property/casualty companies earned an additional $195 million. Canadian life companies earned about $850 million in accident and sickness premiums abroad. PGICs include the Manitoba Public Insurance Corporation, Saskatchewan Government Insurance Office (excluding data from Automobile Accident Insurance Act Division), the Insurance Corporation of British Columbia and the *Régie de l'assurance automobile du Québec*. Lloyds is included in federally registered companies.

STRUCTURE OF THE CANADIAN INSURANCE INDUSTRY

There are slight variations in the list of components which comprise "the insurance industry" in Canada depending on the data source. For example, the reports of the Superintendent of Insurance for Canada exclude provincially registered private companies and provincial government insurance corporations (PGICs), both of which are included (save for the *Régie de l'assurance automobile du Québec*) in the industry as defined by Statistics Canada's input/output system. Statistics Canada's *Financial Institutions* publication excludes all PGICs.

For our purposes, the industry is defined to comprise the components shown in table 2. Only life and property/casualty insurance carriers are in-

Table 3

Relative Size of Insurance Industry Components in Terms of Value Added

Life Insurance	64.6%
Accident and sickness branches of life insurance companies	8.9%
Property and Casualty Insurance	26.5%
Total	100.0%

cluded. Following Statistics Canada's Standard Industrial Classification, independent insurance agents and brokers are included in another industry, not insurance carriers.

The industry includes life insurance (individual and group life insurance policies and annuities, pension asset management), accident and sickness insurance (extended health care and dental insurance, disability insurance—almost 90 percent of which is sold by life companies, the rest by property/casualty companies), and property/casualty insurance (automobile, property, liability, marine, aircraft, et cetera).

In 1985 there were 167 life insurance companies in Canada, of which, 22 were provincially licensed. Mutual life companies, which have no shareholders, earned 62 percent of total life and annuity premium income. Table 3 shows our estimates of the relative size of industry components in terms of value added, based on 1985 data in Statistics Canada's *Financial Institutions.*

In table 3, value added in life insurance is calculated as the sum of wages and salaries, commissions and depreciation on assets held for own use. Value added in accident and sickness branches of life companies and property/casualty is the sum of net income before taxes (including investment income) and wages and salaries. Commissions are excluded because they are paid to another industry, namely, insurance brokers.

The dominance of life insurance over property/casualty is more striking when measured in terms of value added than when measured in premiums. This dominance is partly the result of including commissions of company agents in the insurance carrier industry while excluding property/casualty insurance commissions paid to independent agents and brokers.

INDUSTRIAL GROWTH

Table 4 shows the growth of the insurance industry relative to other industry groups over the past 25 years. Growth is measured in terms of the industry's contribution to GDP at constant prices, where GDP is essentially the same as

Table 4
Growth of GDP by Industry of Origin in Constant Prices

	Percentage of Total 1981 GDP	Average Annual Growth Rates (percent)
Total Economy	100.00	4.39
Total Manufacturing	19.31	4.08
Total Services	60.26	4.67
Finance, Insurance and Real Estate	13.91	4.72
Insurance Carriers	0.46	4.38
Property and Casualty	0.12	2.77
Life Insurance	0.34	5.83

Sources: Statistics Canada, catalogue 15-512, and estimates by the authors for insurance.

value added. Life insurance has enjoyed faster growth than the total economy, manufacturing, FIRE (finance, insurance and real estate), or total services, while property/casualty insurance carriers have had the slowest growth. Insurance carriers, as a whole, have kept pace with the total economy and outpaced manufacturing but not FIRE.

The data show total services growing faster than the rest of the economy despite the fact that the real output growth of services is probably underestimated as a result of measurement problems. The movement of real output in many service industries is based on input measures such as employment.

The measures of output at constant prices for insurance carriers are discussed in detail in chapter 4.

EMPLOYMENT AND WAGES

Table 5 shows the size in 1985 and the growth rate (1961-85) for employment in the insurance industry relative to other industry groups. Employment by insurance carriers is only 1 percent of the total, and insurance employment grew more slowly than the total—at 1.28 percent per year, much more slowly than employment in FIRE (3.47 percent) but faster than for manufacturing (0.51 percent).

Table 6 shows average weekly earnings in the insurance industry and in various other industry groups. Average earnings in the insurance industry exactly kept pace with manufacturing over 1961-85, although there were minor divergences during the period. Average weekly earnings were consistently higher for insurance carriers than for FIRE as a whole, and the growth rate

Table 5

Employment Growth in Insurance Industry

	Number of Employees in 1985	Average Annual Growth Rate
Industrial Aggregate	8,995,197 (100.0%)	1.62%
Manufacturing	1,703,920 (18.9%)	0.51%
FIRE	556,571 (6.2%)	3.47%
Insurance Carriers	90,114 (1.0%)	1.28%

Sources: Statistics Canada ES-1 Survey, 1961-1983, and SEPH Survey, 1983-1985, chain linked in 1983. CANSIM matrices 8003 and 1432.

for both was about 8 percent, slightly faster than for all industries combined at 7.6 percent per year, compounded.

Our results for labour productivity measurement are presented in chapter 4 and will not be repeated here.

INSURANCE PRICES

The consumer price index (CPI) contains three components relevant to insurance: auto insurance, homeowner's insurance and tenant's insurance. There is no component for life insurance in the CPI, but we are able to derive one from our measure of the value of life insurance services at constant prices (chapter 4). The ratio of current value of production to production at constant prices yields an implicit price index for life insurance, which is presented in table 7.

The CPI insurance components measure premium rates which are heavily influenced by claims expense. These CPI components do not measure the value of insurance carrier services alone as our price index for life insurance does.

Table 6
Average Weekly Earnings

Year	FIRE	Industrial Composite	Manufacturing	Insurance Carriers
1961	$ 68.09	$ 78.24	$ 77.83	$ 78.02
1962	70.45	80.54	80.17	81.09
1963	72.58	83.28	82.94	83.83
1964	76.54	86.50	86.29	87.48
1965	82.56	91.01	90.47	94.06
1966	86.97	96.30	95.57	98.51
1967	92.58	102.79	101.68	104.89
1968	99.28	109.92	109.19	110.35
1969	106.43	117.83	117.34	116.33
1970	112.70	126.78	126.70	124.42
1971	121.18	137.65	137.42	135.09
1972	131.66	149.22	149.00	148.19
1973	144.42	160.46	159.86	165.73
1974	161.07	178.09	177.16	184.11
1975	180.59	203.34	203.72	200.86
1976	199.84	228.03	230.21	219.2
1977	214.68	249.95	253.93	236.87
1978	232.31	265.35	272.67	261.22
1979	254.45	288.32	297.03	286.84
1980	284.62	317.39	326.62	317.32
1981	330.76	355.28	366.28	351.61
1982	364.65	390.79	404.99	391.29
1983	396.66	419.51	438.29	426.02
1984	417.69	441.82	465.64	463.16
1985	432.42	457.44	488.14	488.73
Average Annual Growth Rate				
	8.01%	7.64%	7.95%	7.95%

Sources: Statistics Canada ES-1 Survey, 1961-1983, chain linked to SEPH, 1983-1985, with SEPH as a control level. Statistics Canada, catalogue 72-202.

Table 7
Indices of Consumer Prices

Year	Total CPI	Auto Insurance	Tenant Insurance	Homeowner Insurance	Life Insurance
1961	100.00	100.00	100.00	100.00	100.00
1962	101.20	103.28	98.45	101.72	103.45
1963	102.96	103.86	97.94	105.17	103.63
1964	104.82	114.87	102.58	110.95	106.17
1965	107.40	142.08	105.15	117.50	109.46
1966	111.41	154.19	122.16	126.03	116.14
1967	115.38	156.15	128.87	133.62	120.92
1968	120.11	152.55	132.99	143.28	126.41
1969	125.51	156.24	135.05	147.50	138.65
1970	129.74	170.93	136.60	161.90	145.56
1971	133.42	183.44	151.55	198.02	148.15
1972	139.79	191.83	160.31	246.29	154.05
1973	150.43	200.75	174.74	306.38	166.22
1974	166.78	217.89	194.85	348.36	182.88
1975	184.82	259.30	262.89	421.38	196.04
1976	198.69	314.69	328.87	527.24	203.47
1977	214.57	334.53	364.43	605.69	209.10
1978	233.69	327.70	377.84	652.24	229.05
1979	255.06	340.12	394.85	683.02	244.30
1980	281.03	357.04	430.93	734.05	258.45
1981	316.05	443.85	515.46	862.07	271.81
1982	350.18	565.02	606.19	977.59	252.42
1983	370.50	586.64	684.54	1022.41	251.53
1984	386.63	590.19	744.33	1074.14	282.13
1985	401.91	603.37	765.46	1106.03	272.58
Average Annual Growth Rates					
1961–71	2.93%	6.26%	4.24%	7.07%	4.01%
1971–85	8.19%	8.88%	12.26%	13.07%	4.45%

Sources: Statistics Canada (CPI) and the authors' estimate for life insurance.

The price of the average homeowner insurance policy grew more rapidly than any other type of insurance over 1961-85 (partly as a result of rising house prices), followed by the price of the average tenant's policy. Auto insurance prices grew less quickly, followed by life insurance. The price of life insurance services grew less quickly than the total of all items in the CPI, in contrast to the three CPI insurance components which all grew faster than inflation. To repeat, these results largely reflect the unfavourable trend in claims of property/casualty insurance, although they also reflect the differences in productivity between property/casualty and life insurance carriers (as will be discussed in chapter 4).

Chapter 3

Demand for Insurance Services

INTRODUCTION

In this chapter we analyse the demand for insurance services. First, we present an analysis in the form of an overview of the demand for insurance in Canada, distinguishing between final demand by households and government versus intermediate demand by various industries. We also analyse the available export and import data, explaining the conventions of balance of payments estimates which underlie the data. Secondly, we provide a theoretical framework which shows that consumer demand for insurance can be treated in a parallel manner to demand for any other commodity. Thirdly, we present some original results from an analysis of the 1982 Family Expenditure Survey data on household purchases of insurance services. Lastly, we present an original analysis of aggregate time series data on consumer demand for insurance services in the context of a complete model of demand behaviour.

INDUSTRIAL DEMAND FOR INSURANCE SERVICES

Statistics Canada's input/output tables provide an ideal framework for an overview of insurance commodity supply and demand. In the Canadian system, input/output tables are rectangular (commodity-by-industry) matrices showing production of commodities by industries and use of commodities as inputs in the production process (intermediate demand) or as deliveries to final demand (consumption, government purchases, capital investment, and exports). Each industry can produce more than one commodity, and each commodity can be produced by more than one industry.

There is only one insurance commodity (number 556) in the input/output system and only one business sector industry which produces it. The commodity is insurance services and encompasses life insurance, property/liability and health insurance (including the health insurance services of private companies but not those health insurance services provided by government) and the services of workmen's compensation boards (WCB). The latter is supplied by the government sector. Hence, WCB is part of the insurance commodity but is not produced by the insurance industry. The insurance activities of government business enterprises (PGICs) which are the Insurance Corporation of B.C., Saskatchewan Government Insurance Corporation and the Manitoba Public Insurance Corporation (but not the *Régie de l'assurance automobile du Québec*) are included in the business sector, not in general government.

More than 90 percent of the insurance commodity is provided by the domestic business sector (insurance carriers, industry 169); imports provide most of the remainder and the rest, a small proportion in the form of production by general government of insurance services (WCB), is valued at cost. See table 8 for the breakdown of supply which shows a trend over the period 1961-84 of a rising proportion of imports and of government sector production.

Within the Canadian system of national accounts, life insurance services are valued in terms of the operating costs of producing them. Property/casualty insurance services are valued as the difference between net premiums earned and net claims paid. (See chapter 4 for a detailed analysis of the important question of measuring output.) Investment income is excluded from output of property/casualty insurance, so this component of the industry usually has negative profits. In our opinion, this way of measuring output is faulty. We mention it here to remind the reader that the data presented in table 8 under-represent the value of the insurance commodity by about 10 percent and slightly overstate the variability of production over time.

Table 8 provides a breakdown of demand as well as supply. An almost steady 50 percent is purchased by consumers who purchase all life insurance. Government takes less than 1 percent, and exports have absorbed a proportion which has almost doubled from 2.78 percent in 1961 to 5.37 percent in 1984. The ratio of exports to imports has fallen since 1966.

Intermediate demand is broken down in table 8 by industry group. The finance, insurance and real estate industry includes real estate rental, the corporate owners of residential and commercial property. It is not surprising to see that this is the largest source of demand.

The relative decline in insurance demand by the primary sector (agriculture, forestry, fishing, trapping, mining, quarrying and oil wells) is attributable to the relative decline in the size of this sector. Similarly, we see the effects of the decline in manufacturing activity since 1976. Total intermediate demand fell from 1961 to 1966 but remained stable after that.

Table 8

Supply and Disposition of Insurance Services in the Canadian Economy

	1961	1966	1971	1976	1981	1984
Source of Supply						
Domestic private sector	96.99%	97.08%	94.59%	93.88%	90.82%	91.65%
Government sector	1.17	1.46	1.39	1.71	1.91	1.77
Imports	1.84	1.46	4.02	4.41	7.26	6.59
Total supply	100.00	100.00	100.00	100.00	100.00	100.00
Disposition of intermediate inputs						
Primary sector	3.72%	2.92%	2.65%	2.17%	1.86%	1.90%
Manufacturing	3.72	3.09	3.85	3.04	2.36	2.31
Construction	2.70	2.33	2.17	2.02	1.57	1.29
Transport, communication and utilities	5.05	4.58	4.21	3.40	2.71	2.41
Finance, insurance and real estate	25.56	23.88	25.79	27.98	28.71	31.24
Retail, wholesale and other services	7.01	5.82	4.92	4.84	3.52	3.59
Total intermediate demand	47.76	42.61	43.58	43.44	40.73	42.75
Final demand						
Consumer	48.77%	53.94%	51.76%	52.08%	52.22%	50.95%
Government	0.68	0.80	0.85	0.95	0.77	0.93
Exports	2.78	2.65	3.80	3.53	6.28	5.37
Total final demand	52.24	57.39	56.42	56.56	59.27	57.25
Total demand = total supply	100.00%	100.00%	100.00%	100.00%	100.00%	100.00%
Total, millions of current$	$898	$1,249	$2,092	$4,311	$6,184	$8,396
Ratio of exports to imports	1.52	1.82	0.95	0.80	0.87	0.82

Source: Statistics Canada, Input/Output Accounts.

The input/output framework provides an overview of the demand for insurance. An analysis of consumer demand is given later in this chapter. Before turning to that, exports and imports will be discussed more fully.

TREATMENT OF INSURANCE IN CANADA'S BALANCE OF PAYMENTS

The value of insurance services forms two unpublished components within the Current Account of Canada's Balance of Payment (BOP), items A23/B23, Other Service Receipts/Payments. A23/B23 comprises transactions by governments not included elsewhere in the accounts, miscellaneous income, and business services and other transactions. The latter two contain elements of trade in insurance services. The net revenues of Canadian insurance companies from insurance operations abroad and the corresponding payment item are in miscellaneous income. These items have a large (but indeterminable) element of payment to head office for management, accounting, and other services; so, despite the fact that the remaining part of net revenues are factor payments, these items are classified as services. Part of the net revenue of Canadian head offices from operations abroad is branch profits earned abroad (branches are not incorporated as foreign subsidiaries abroad). These are recorded on an accrual, not a payments, basis; this constitutes an exception to standard practice in the BOP.

The bulk of insurance transactions are property/casualty and marine premiums net of claims, classified to business services and other transactions. Much of these insurance premiums are earned on goods shipped abroad and, correspondingly, on imported goods which are insured in transit. Additional transactions are related to re-insurance, with major international re-insurers being located abroad.

Canadian life insurance companies, in their global operations, earned about $5.6 billion or 40 percent of their premium income abroad in 1985 (CLHIA *Facts*). These figures do not appear in the Canadian BOP except as described above, because the premiums are largely earned by subsidiaries abroad and as such are transactions between a non-resident institution and non-resident individuals. The great success of Canadian life companies abroad is little reflected in the balance of payments.

The BOP presentation of insurance transactions is not completely consistent with the rest of the Canadian System of National Accounts (CSNA). In the rest of the CSNA, life insurance is valued in terms of the associated operating expenses, not as premiums less claims. The reserves of both life companies and property/casualty companies are treated as assets of policyholders in the CSNA. No such record is made in the capital account of the BOP for transactions between residents and non-residents. The data requirements may be forbidding, but it would seem appropriate to render BOP treatment consistent with the rest of the CSNA. Finally, we note that our proposal to include imputed interest in the value of property/casualty insurance premiums (as discussed in chapter 4) should be carried over to the BOP.

CONSUMERS' INSURANCE DECISIONS

Individuals face risks which can lead to loss of property, loss of ability to earn income and, in the extreme, loss of life. It is possible for an individual to insure against these events, at least to a certain extent. An insurance firm pools the risks of individuals and thereby is able to offer contingent claims or policies against various losses.

The decision to purchase insurance is like any consumption/portfolio decision (see Ehrlich and Becker 1972). The variety and quantity of insurance purchased reflects the consumer's preferences, expectations, income, the prices of insurance policies and the prices of other commodities. A simple model will serve to highlight the insurance decision. Suppose an individual purchases two commodities, insurance and non-insurance or consumption. The quantity of the latter is x_1 and for simplicity the price is always normalized to \$1. The nominal or dollar value of insurance is represented by z. The individual also has nominal income, y. Insurance is purchased in order to protect against loss of family income. In this example, the insurance policy is related to disability or loss of life. If the individual lives or is not disabled (i.e., state of nature 1) the family budget constraint is

(1) $x_1 + z = y$

However, if the individual suffers a loss of income (i.e., state of nature 2) then the budget constraint is

(2) $x_2 + z = bz$

where x_2 is the quantity of consumption when loss of income occurs (there is no reason for $x_1 = x_2$), $b > 1$ is the benefits received per dollar of insurance. The budget constraints can be pictured quite easily if we combine the two equations by solving for z in (2) and then substitute into (1). Thus

(3) $x_1 + x_2 / (b\text{-}1) = y$

If $x_2 = 0$, then $x_1 = y$. All the income is devoted to consumption when no disability or loss of life occurs. If $x_1 = 0$, then $x_2 = y(b\text{-}1)$. Recall that if $x_1 = 0$, then $z = y$. So all income is spent on insurance and $x_2 = z(b\text{-}1)$ with $z(b\text{-}1)$ defined as the net income to be devoted to consumption when disability or loss of life occurs.

For given income (y) and per dollar insurance benefits (b), when x_1 increases by one unit then x_2 must decrease by (b-1). This can be seen from equation 3. For a given level of income, any increase in consumption in the first state of nature (x_1) in which no loss is suffered means a sacrifice of (b-1) units of consumption in the second state of nature (x_2) in which the loss is suffered. Geometrically, in figure 1, y is represented by point A, y(b-1) is given by point B.

Equations 1 and 2 or just 3 represent the constraints under which an individual has to make decisions. In order to make decisions, however, an individual must have an objective. The objective represents the preferences or tastes of the individual, and it can be written down as

(4) $u = qU(x_1) + (1\text{-}q)U(x_2)$

where U is the preference or utility function which shows how an individual values consumption and U is increasing in x_1 and x_2, q is the probability that there will not be any disability or loss of life, so (1-q) is the probability that the individual will suffer a loss of income, and u represents the expected utility of consumption under the two possible events. An individual decides how much to consume and purchases insurance by maximizing expected utility, subject to the constraints.

It is possible to trace the trade-off between x_1 and x_2 according to the individual's preference in the same manner that we performed this task for the constraint faced by the individual. If expected utility (u) and probability (q) are fixed, then an increase in x_1 leads to an increase in utility (U) by $qU'(x_1)$. The ′ denotes the marginal or incremental increase in U due to an increase in x_1. In order to keep expected utility fixed, x_2 must decrease. This decrease causes utility to decline by $(1\text{-}q)U'(x_2)$. Thus the trade-off of x_2 for x_1 is $qU'(x_1) / (1\text{-}q)U'(x_2)$. The curve in figure 1 shows the preferences of the individual, and the slope of the curve denotes the trade-off between consumption with and without the loss in income according to these preferences.

In order to obtain the highest level of preference satisfaction possible given the budget constraints, the individual equates the preference trade-off between x_2 and x_1 to the market trade-off given by the budget constraints. This means that the individual is willing to give up the same amount of x_1 for an additional unit of x_2 as the market dictates. Hence, the condition is

$$(5)\quad \frac{qU'(x_1)}{(1\text{-}q)U'(x_2)} = (b\text{-}1)$$

Geometrically, point E in figure 1 shows the quantities of x_1^* and x_2^* demanded by the individual. In addition, the difference between points A and x_1^* shows the amount of insurance purchased by the individual per dollar of

Figure 1
Individual Insurance Consumption Decision

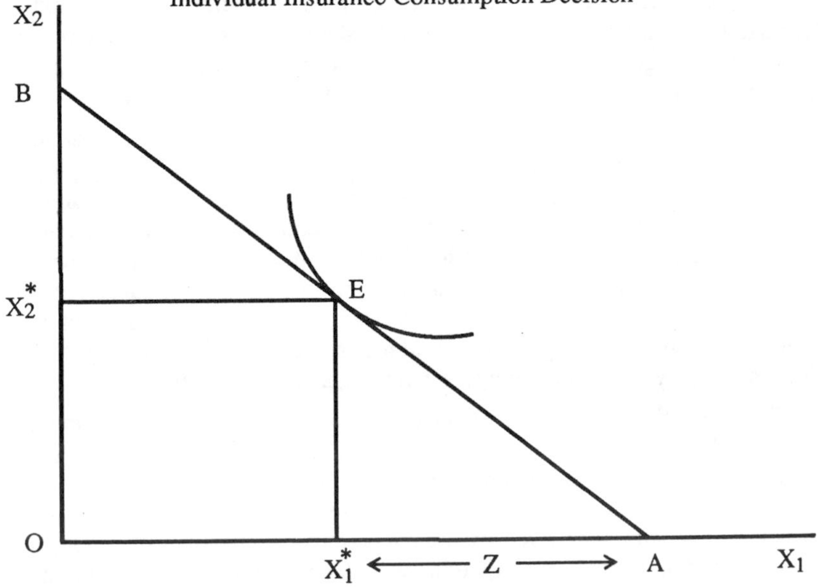

consumption. This can be seen from the budget constraint given by equation 1 where $y\text{-}x_1 = z$.

Clearly, the amount of insurance purchased by the individual depends on the income level, the gross benefit rate, the probability of the insured against the event not occurring and the preferences (U) of the individual. It is important to recognize that the demand for insurance is similar to and imbedded within the demand decisions for all other commodities.

CROSS-SECTIONAL ANALYSIS OF HOUSEHOLD DEMAND FOR INSURANCE

Statistics Canada's *Survey of Family Expenditure in Canada, 1982* (catalogue 62-555) provides a rich database for the analysis of household expenditure patterns. The survey was based on a household sample designed to represent the entire nation's spending in calendar year 1982. A public use data tape with complete records for 10,938 spending units (families and unattached individuals) is available from Statistics Canada. The following analysis is based on that set of records.

Consumer response to price variation is analysed in another section of this study using time series data in which all types of insurance are aggregated into a single category. In this section, we exploit disaggregated data, but for our purposes the available data are limited in significant respects. Respondents to the family expenditure survey are asked to report expenditure on the following categories of insurance: homeowner's insurance, tenant's insurance, life insurance, health insurance, and automobile insurance.

Unfortunately, the important category of auto insurance is not separately recorded on the public use data tape. It is also important to note that employer payments for life and health insurance are excluded. So, for example, employer contributions to group life and extended health care insurance plans are not reported; on the other hand, employee contributions to the government health care plan in Ontario are reported as part of consumer expenditure, whereas in some other provinces health care is funded entirely from tax revenues. Owing to these limitations, we confine our analysis to the first three categories: homeowner's, tenant's, and life insurance.

The family expenditure data on insurance record premium payments, whereas the national accounts data on personal consumer expenditure record either the sales and administrative expenses (in the case of life insurance) or the net of premiums less claims (in the case of property and casualty insurance). The administrative expenses of government health insurance plans are recorded in government expenditure in the national accounts, not in personal consumption expenditure. As a result of these differences, the family expenditure and the national accounts data used in the time series demand analysis are not directly comparable.

Table 9 shows the percentage of households reporting expenditure on tenant, homeowner and life insurance and average dollar expenditure in 1982. Nearly all homeowners (94.5 percent) purchase insurance on their property, and the average annual premium for those who do was $240.05 in 1982. By contrast, less than half of all tenants (48.6 percent) buy insurance. Insurance on rental property is purchased by the landlord, not the tenant. Tenant insurance covers contents, theft and liability. In view of the more limited coverage of tenant's insurance, it is surprising that the average premium, at $232.42, is nearly as high as for homeowner's policies. This is likely because only high income tenants buy insurance whereas nearly all homeowners do.

One possible explanation for the very high incidence of purchase of insurance by homeowners is that insurance is required by mortgage companies. This argument is undermined by the observation that nearly half (47.5 percent) of homeowners report no mortgage. Homeowners purchase insurance to protect their assets, namely their homes, whether or not these assets are owned in part by mortgage companies. Tenants are in a different position with respect to protecting the buildings they occupy.

Table 9

Consumer Expenditure on Selected Categories of Insurance

	Average Expenditure All Households (in dollars)	Percentage of All Households Reporting Expenditure	Percentage of Owner Households Reporting Expenditure	Percentage of Tenant Households Reporting Expenditure	Average of Those Reporting Expenditure (in dollars)
Homeowners' Insurance	$ 139.95	58.3%	94.5%		$240.05
Tenants' Insurance	43.23	18.6		48.6	232.42
Subtotal	183.18	76.9			472.47
Life Insurance	218.76	50.7			431.48
Total Services	$ 5,739.12	100.0%			
Total Expenditure	21,900.48	100.0			

Sources: Statistics Canada, Survey of Family Expenditures, 1982, Public Use Data Tape, and estimates by the authors.

Average life insurance premiums are $431.48 for the 50.7 percent of households reporting this category of expenditure. These figures are understatements because they exclude employer contributions to group plans. In the national accounts, employer contributions are part of both labour income and consumer expenditure.

The average household expenditure on services ($5,739.12) and average total expenditure ($21,900.48) are our own estimates, created for a larger study, which are designed to be as consistent as possible with national accounts definitions while satisfying consistent aggregation of both time series and cross-sectional data. We estimate imputed rent on owner-occupied dwellings and include this in the durables category of expenditure. Investment in housing stock (e.g. renovations) is excluded from current consumption. Repair services for durables and semi-durables are included in "services," whereas in the national accounts they are in durables or semi-durables, respectively.

Household expenditure data are often studied in order to determine the relationship between expenditure on a particular category and total income (or total expenditure). This relationship is usually referred to as an Engel function, after the nineteenth-century pioneer German researcher on household budget data. The response of specific expenditures to income is of interest, among other reasons, for forecasting changes in specific expendi-

Table 10

Engel Functions and Income Elasticities for Insurance and Services

Category of Expenditure	Mean Share (w)	Estimated Coefficients (standard errors) (a)	(b)	Income Elasticity (at mean)	Class of Commodity
All services	0.2509	−0.1494 (.0165)	0.0407 (.0017)	1.16	Luxury
Non-insurance services	0.2257	−0.1184 (.0162)	0.0349 (.0016)	1.15	Luxury
Property insurance (homeowners + tenants)	0.0087	0.0183 (.0024)	−0.00097 (.00024)	0.89	Necessity
Life insurance	0.0086	−0.0428 (.0024)	0.0052 (.0002)	1.60	Luxury

Source: Authors' estimates.

tures as incomes rise in the future. The income elasticity of demand measures the ratio of the percentage change in quantity purchased to the percentage change in income. A negative elasticity value corresponds to decreased expenditure with rising income, and such goods are labelled "inferior." Goods displaying a positive income elasticity but less than 1.0 are labelled "necessities," while goods with elasticities greater than 1.0 are "luxuries." The share of the latter in total expenditure rises with income.

A variety of functional forms are commonly used to estimate Engel functions. One of the most popular is the following:

(6) $w_i = a_i + b_i \ln y$

where wi is the i-th expenditure share or fraction of total expenditure going to the i-th commodity, a_i and b_i are constants and $\ln y$ is the natural logarithm of total household expenditure. If b_i is greater than zero, the expenditure share rises with income and the commodity is a "luxury."

Table 10 reports results from the estimation of equations of form (6) for various categories of expenditure. Services as a group constitute a quarter of total expenditure on average and are a luxury, with an income elasticity of 1.16. The elasticity itself falls with rising income; in other words, the income elasticity is higher for low income families. This observation holds true for all categories in table 10 and is a consequence of the functional form chosen. Services excluding all reported insurance expenditure (i.e., excluding all insurance save auto insurance) are reported on line two of table 10. The results are naturally little different from "all services." Property insurance, which combines homeowner's and tenant's insurance, has an income elasticity of 0.89 and is therefore a "necessity." The life insurance category shows the most extreme results with an income elasticity of demand of 1.60, a strong "luxury."

Based on these results, one would forecast well above average growth in life insurance premiums as income grows in the future but below average growth for property insurance. However, the analysis to this point neglects the effects of demographic variables. One would like to know how expenditure varies across households which differ in characteristics such as household size, age of household head, region, urban versus rural, sex of household head, tenure. We next turn to this analysis.

Our sample size is sufficiently large at 10,938 that it is feasible to estimate Engel functions, with many dummy variables representing demographic characteristics, in the following form:

(7) $w = a + b \ln y + c_1D_1 + c_2D_2 + \ldots c_nD_n$

where w, a, b, ln y are defined as in equation 6 with the subscript i, which refers to the expenditure category, suppressed; c_j and D_j (j=1 to n) are regression coefficients and dummy variables, respectively. Each dummy variable takes on the value 1 when a household displays the relevant characteristic ($D_j = 0$ otherwise). The coefficient c_j therefore measures the way that expenditure shares vary across demographic groups. We note that this functional form has the advantage of permitting exact aggregation in the pooling of cross-sectional and time series data (see Jorgenson, Lau and Stoker 1982), a topic beyond the scope of this monograph but noted here as a justification for the functional form in (7). Table 11 shows the results of estimating Engel functions of the form in (7) and defines the dummy variables that were used.

In each of the regressions reported in table 11 (all services, property insurance, life insurance) the reference demographic group is a 25-34 year old male-headed household, with two persons living in a metropolitan area (population greater than 30,000) in Ontario and owning their own home. Setting all dummy variables in the equation equal to zero will yield the relationship between expenditure share and income for the reference demographic group. The independent and additive impacts of the characteristics measured by the dummy variables are then easily read from the coefficient columns in table 11. Each coefficient measures the percentage change in expenditure share resulting from the presence of the associated characteristic.

For example, under "all services" it is seen that according to the model, female-headed households' expenditure share on services is 1.07 percent

Table 11
Engel Functions with Demographic Variables
(all coefficients multiplied by 100)

Variable and Definition	Units with Characteristic (percent)	All Services Coefficient	All Services Standard Error	Property Insurance Coefficient	Property Insurance Standard Error	Life Insurance Coefficient	Life Insurance Standard Error
a = constant		–41.67	2.25	1.894	0.337	–9.150	0.335
b = coefficient of lnY (log expenditure)		6.97	2.19	–0.100	0.033	0.203	0.033
F = 1 if head is female	28.1	–1.07	0.22	0.092	0.033	–0.214	0.033
A1 = 1 if age of head is under 25	7.1	–0.29	0.39	–0.225	0.059	–0.234	0.058
A3 = 1 if age of head is 35–44	20.2	–1.33	0.28	0.041	0.042	–0.013	0.041
A4 = 1 if age of head is 45–54	15.7	–1.69	0.29	0.025	0.044	–0.244	0.044
A5 = 1 if age of head is 55–64	14.3	–2.11	0.31	0.124	0.046	–0.317	0.046
A6 = 1 if age of head is 65 +	17.3	–2.86	0.31	0.286	0.047	–0.539	0.047
S1 = 1 if household size is 1	21.3	4.92	0.29	–0.013	0.043	–0.105	0.043
S3 = 1 if household size is 3	17.6	–0.81	0.28	–0.050	0.042	0.105	0.041
S4 = 1 if household size is 4	18.4	–2.45	0.29	–0.056	0.044	0.209	0.043
S5 = 1 if household size is 5 +	13.2	–3.69	0.33	–0.168	0.049	0.127	0.049
PD1 = 1 if farm	2.0	–2.11	0.65	0.481	0.097	–0.056	–0.096
PD2 = 1 if non-farm, non-metro (less than 30,000)	17.9	–0.97	0.25	0.039	0.037	–0.117	0.036
REG1 = 1 if in Atlantic provinces	19.7	–1.49	0.28	–0.058	0.042	–0.039	0.042
REG2 = 1 if in Quebec	19.6	–0.54	0.28	0.572	0.041	0.498	0.041
REG4 = 1 if in Prairie provinces	24.6	–1.03	0.26	–0.095	0.039	–0.025	0.039
REG5 = 1 if in B.C., Yukon, N.W. Territories	12.4	–2.17	0.32	–0.068	0.047	–0.216	0.047
T = 1 if a tenant	38.3	2.47	0.22	–0.447	0.033	–0.137	0.033
Expenditure share (Mean × 100)		25.09		0.87		0.86	
Income elasticity		1.28		0.89		1.24	

Source: Authors' estimates.

lower than for male-headed households with otherwise similar characteristics. The service share falls steadily with age of household head except for the youngest group which is slightly lower than the 25-34 year old age group. Service share falls monotonically with household size and the effect is pronounced, showing a range of 8.61 percentage points. Inhabitants of larger urban areas spend more on services and Ontarians spend more than otherwise similar households in other provinces (B.C. appears to be the lowest). Tenants spend 2.47 percentage points more on services than do homeowners.

Turning now to property insurance, the more notable patterns are the following: the expenditure share increases with age of household head but decreases with household size; farm households spend much more on property insurance and tenants much less (not surprisingly, given the results in table 9); and Quebec residents spend much more.

Female-headed households spend a lower share on life insurance than male-headed households, and the 25-34 year old age group spends more than any other age group. Larger households tend to spend more on life insurance, the reverse of the trend for property insurance. Quebec residents spend more on both life and property insurance. Tenants spend less than homeowners on both types of insurance.

Two of the three income elasticities are different as a result of including the 17 dummy variables in the model. The income elasticity for all services rises from 1.16 to 1.28 when the dummies are added, whereas the income elasticity for life insurance falls from 1.60 to 1.24. The income elasticity for property insurance is unchanged at 0.89. Services and life insurance remain classified as luxury goods; property insurance is a necessity.

These results on demographic variables are interesting in themselves, but they gain in significance when combined with time series data showing the relative growth rates of incomes of different demographic groups. A full analysis is beyond the scope of this study, but a few results can be sketched. The income share of female-headed households has been growing relative to male-headed households in recent years because of growth in the relative number of the former. If this trend continues into the future, then the results in table 10 imply a negative effect on services' expenditure share and on life insurance as well, but a small positive effect on property insurance. Similarly, the aging of the population of household heads in conjunction with our regression results imply a decreasing share for services and life insurance, but an increasing expenditure share for property insurance. The trend to single person households will increase the services share and decrease the life insurance share.

TIME SERIES EVIDENCE FOR HOUSEHOLD DEMAND FOR INSURANCE

The demand for insurance by households is determined in a similar fashion and in conjunction with the demand for other commodities. In deciding on their commodity demands, individuals maximize the objective of preference satisfaction subject to their budget constraints. The latter is defined by the prices of commodities and level of income. Numerous models of consumer demand have been developed in the literature (see Phlips 1983 and Deaton and Muellbauer 1983). Recent work has emphasized that consumer or household demand decisions should be modelled as an interrelated system of equations which is sufficiently flexible so as not to rule out empirically significant effects of price and income changes. In this section we estimate a system of consumer demand equations (based on a translogarithmic expenditure function). This model is also referred to as the almost ideal demand system (see Deaton and Muellbauer 1980). Our formulation relates to the decisions on consumer durables, semi-durables, non-durables, non-insurance services and insurance services.

The equation system estimated was

$$(8) \qquad s_i = a_i + \sum_{j=1}^{5} a_{ij} \ln(p_j/y) + b_i \ln y - b_i\left(\sum_{j=1}^{5} a_j \ln(p_j/y) + .5\sum_{k=1}^{5}\sum_{j=1}^{5} a_{kj} \ln(p_k/y)\ln(p_j/y)\right)$$

$$\text{with} \sum_{j=1}^{5} a_j = 1, \sum_{j=1}^{5} a_{ij} = 0, i=1,\ldots,5, \sum_{j=1}^{5} b_j = 0.$$

The variable si is the expenditure share of the ith commodity, which is pixi/y where pi is the price, xi is the quantity and y is nominal income, and the a's and b's are unknown parameters which have to be estimated.

Data

Data for the time series analysis are constructed from Statistic Canada's national income and expenditure accounts and from our own estimates of the value of service flows from the stock of consumer durables. The consumer durables stocks are estimated by the Financial Flows Section of Statistics Canada. For our purposes, aggregate personal consumption expenditure comprises five categories: durables, semi-durables, non-durable goods, insurance services, and non-insurance services. A total of 130 component price series are aggregated into Divisia price indexes and constant dollar quantities for these five categories. The sample period is 1952-82.

The categorization of the 130 component series is the same as Statistics Canada's gross national expenditure (GNE) categories for personal consumption expenditure, with the following major exceptions. Both cash and imputed rent are included in our estimates of consumption of durables, whereas they are included in expenditure on services in the GNE accounts. All repair services are included in our category of non-insurance services, whereas in the GNE accounts repair services for durable goods are included in the durables category and repair services for semi-durable goods are included in semi-durables. Finally, a few items (tableware, kitchenware, hardware, lamps, fixtures) which are included in the semi-durables category in the GNE accounts are classified as durables in our data in order to be consistent with the Financial Flow Accounts estimates of the stocks of consumer durables.

The rental value of each subcategory of durables is defined to be equal to the depreciation plus the opportunity cost of funds invested in the stock, defined as the rate of interest times the value of the stock. Depreciation and stock estimates were provided by the Financial Flows Section.

Insurance services comprise expenditures on the following GNE categories: property insurance, theft insurance, accident and sickness insurance, auto insurance, and life insurance. Consistent with national accounts' conventions, non-life insurance expenditures are defined as premiums net of claims; life insurance expenditures are defined as the commissions and general expenses of providing life insurance.

The estimation results are presented in table 12. The fit was good and the majority of parameter estimates were statistically significant. Table 13 shows the effect of a 1 percent increase in income on the demands for non-durables, semi-durables, durables, non-insurance services and insurance services. We find that services respond relatively more to income changes than do the other commodity groups. Moreover, within services, insurance exhibits a larger income effect than non-insurance services. Indeed, the demand for insurance is the most elastic compared to other demands. A 1 percent increase in income causes the demand for insurance to increase by 1.5 percent on average over the period 1952 to 1982. This figure is in line with the income effects obtained in the cross-section analysis.

Because prices change over time for each commodity group, and since the demand for each commodity is a function of its own price and the price of the other commodities, time series data within the context of our model permits us to investigate the various "own" and "cross" price effects. Table 14 shows

Table 12
Estimation Results

Parameter*	Estimate	Standard Error
a_1	0.266	0.084
a_2	0.071	0.009
a_3	0.331	0.020
a_5	0.022	0.012
b_1	0.084	0.004
b_2	–0.026	0.002
b_3	–0.067	0.004
a_{11}	–0.022	0.049
a_{22}	0.038	0.003
a_{33}	0.057	0.011
a_{55}	–0.008	0.092

Equation	Standard Error
Non-Insurance	0.022
Semi-Durables	0.003
Non-Durables	0.005
Insurance Services	0.005
Log of Likelihood Function	478.258

Source: Authors' estimates.
Note: *Could not reject the hypotheses that $b_5 = 0$ and $a_{ij} = 0$ for $i \neq j$.

Table 13
Income Effects on Household Demand for Five Commodity Groups

	Non-Durables	Semi-Durables	Durables*	Non-Insurance Services	Insurance Services
1952	0.84	0.82	1.00	1.32	1.63
1957	0.83	0.79	1.00	1.29	1.53
1962	0.82	0.79	1.00	1.28	1.53
1967	0.81	0.79	1.00	1.26	1.50
1972	0.82	0.79	1.00	1.25	1.49
1977	0.80	0.74	1.00	1.23	1.43
1982	0.78	0.69	1.00	1.23	1.38

Source: Authors' estimates.
Note: * Could not reject the hypothesis that the income effect on durables was 1.00.

Table 14

Own Price Effects on Household Demand for Five Commodity Groups

	Non-Durables	Semi-Durables	Durables	Non-Insurance Services	Insurance Services
1952	−0.79	−0.71	−0.60	−1.16	−1.51
1957	−0.78	−0.68	−0.65	−1.15	−1.43
1962	−0.77	−0.67	−0.65	−1.14	−1.43
1967	−0.76	−0.66	−0.64	−1.13	−1.39
1972	−0.76	−0.67	−0.64	−1.12	−1.43
1982	−0.72	−0.52	−0.69	−1.11	−1.30

Source: Authors' estimates.

the own price effects on commodity demand. Each column shows the effect of a 1 percent increase in the price of a commodity on the demand for that commodity. Demands for services are the most responsive to changes in their respective prices. A 1 percent increase in the prices of semi-durables and durables generated decreases in their respective demands by about -0.65 percent on average over the period 1952 to 1982. The demand for non-durables was slightly more price responsive than the other two groups, with an average price effect of 0.75 percent. The demand for insurance services was the most price responsive. On average over the period, a 1 percent increase in the price for insurance services caused the demand for insurance to decline by 1.40 percent. The average price effect for non-insurance services was about 1.15 percent. Hence, we find that as commodities are less durable they become more price responsive.

Besides responding to their own prices, each of the demands also responds to the prices of the other commodities. These effects are the so-called cross price effects. The importance of these measures is that they show the degree to which commodities are substitutes or complements. If an increase in the price of commodity i causes an increase in the demand for commodity j, then the two commodities are substitutes. Households substitute the relatively cheaper commodity for the one which is relatively more expensive. If an increase in the price of commodity i leads to a decrease in the demand for commodity j, then the two commodities are complements. The cross price effects (more precisely the partial substitution elasticities of compensated demand) are presented in table 15. From this table we find that all the commodities are substitutes except durables and semi-durables. These two commodities are complements. Insurance services are substitutable for all other commodities. Hence, as the price of all non-insurance commodities increases they become more valuable and therefore the demand for insurance expands.

Table 15

Cross Price Effects on Household Demand for Five Commodity Groups

Commodities	Average Cross Effect
Non-durables—Semi-durables	1.05
Non-durables—Durables	0.13
Non-durables—Non-insurance service	0.95
Non-durables—Insurance services	0.91
Semi-durables—Durables	–0.78
Semi-durables—Non-insurance services	0.94
Semi-durables—Insurance services	0.88
Durables—Non-insurance services	1.39
Durables—Insurance services	3.10
Non-insurance services—Insurance services	1.11

Source: Authors' estimates.

SUMMARY

Households purchase over half of all insurance services. About 5 percent goes to exports and the bulk of the remainder is purchased as intermediate inputs by industry, chiefly finance insurance and real estate. This chapter has focused on an analysis of consumer or household demand for insurance services using both cross-sectional data and time series data. Demand analysis is an essential component of an attempt to understand the forces driving industry growth—its past and future prospects.

Cross-sectional data from Statistics Canada's 1982 Family Expenditure Survey provide some detail on the relationship between demand, income and household characteristics, but no information on price effects. This is analysed using time series data. Both cross-sectional and time series analysis show total insurance services to be "luxury" goods (i.e., income elasticity greater than one). The cross-sectional data reveal a higher income elasticity for life insurance than property insurance, with the latter less than one, at 0.89. Separate data on auto insurance is unavailable. Demand for property insurance rises with age of household head while demand for life insurance falls. The reverse pattern holds for size of household, with demand for property insurance falling with size of household and demand for life insurance rising. Female household heads spend more on property insurance and less on life insurance than males. Tenant households spend much less on property insurance and somewhat less on life insurance than homeowner households do. Demand for both types of insurance is significantly higher in Quebec than in other provinces.

Time series evidence for the period 1952-82 shows the price responsiveness of demand for insurance services to be higher than for any other category of consumer expenditure. Price elasticity of demand increases as we move from durables to semi-durables, to non-durables, to non-insurance services, to insurance services. Cross price effects are also estimated, revealing that insurances' services are substitutable for other services, non-durables, semi-durables and durables.

These results have important implications for the growth of the insurance industry. First, the high income elasticity of demand which we estimate for the industry as a whole from both cross-sectional and time series analysis implies a secular trend which is higher than the growth rate of income but which is also subject to sharper fluctuations as income fluctuates, always assuming relative prices constant. Secondly, the high price elasticity of demand implies a strong negative impact on demand and sales revenues from rising prices of insurance services, and vice versa. Thirdly, there are significant demographic effects on demand from the changing sex and age distribution of household heads, household size, et cetera. Finally, we find that durables and insurance services are strong substitutes—as the price of durables rises (and they become more valuable) the demand for insurance rises.

Chapter 4

Production and Cost of Insurance Services

INTRODUCTION

The purpose of this chapter is to discuss the structure of production of insurance services. In particular, we want to focus on the measurement issues relating to outputs and inputs and the estimates pertaining to scale economies, scope economies, factor substitution and productivity growth.

There are also significant policy concerns which arise from an analysis of the "supply side." These concerns centre on the efficiency implications of mergers within the insurance industry and between insurance firms and firms in other industries in the financial sector. For example, a solution to the potential problem of excess concentration in financial markets would entail a prohibition against offering many different services in the financial sector. However, it is also asserted that there are incentives through economies of scope (or diversity) to become a financial conglomerate. The empirical evidence of scope economies highlights whether there are cost incentives to conglomeration or whether the conglomerates may be a vehicle for collusion and therefore monopolization.

OUTPUT MEASUREMENT

A great deal of controversy and confusion surrounds the nature of the outputs provided by insurance firms. Individuals, or in general any purchasers of insurance, actually buy financial protection. An insurance firm is able to offer protection because it has created the facilities for pooling risks. Insurance firms do not bear the risk of their purchasers; they pool the risk. Thus, insurance companies actually provide financial intermediation. It is the range of activities an insurance company undertakes as part of its efforts to pool risks that constitutes the services provided by the company.

To understand more clearly what we mean, consider for example a brokerage firm dealing in corporate bonds. Because of various information asymmetries and economies of specialization, corporations sell their bonds through a broker. Individuals (or any other type of purchaser) buy the bonds from the broker, not directly from the issuer. Let's assume the broker buys one kind of bond at $98 each and sells it for $100. What is the output of the broker and the price of that output? The broker provides the facilities to buy and sell bonds, an intermediary function. The revenue from the intermediary role is ($100 – $98)n, where n is the number of bonds sold. Hence, $2 n is the revenue which must cover (in the long run) the current and capital costs of the brokerage function. In this example, it is relatively easy to determine the revenues and costs of bond brokerage.

Our example fits neatly into the context of insurance, $100 is the premium, $98 is the claim and n is the number of term life insurance contracts (there is assumed to be, for the moment, only one kind of policy). Thus $2 n is the revenue from risk pooling. This concept of revenues related to the intermediation roles of insurance has not often been used in empirical studies of insurance, but Geehan (1977), Hirshhorn and Geehan (1977), and Kellner and Mathewson (1983) are notable exceptions.

The decomposition of insurance revenues into price and quantity components is quite difficult. For example, with revenues of $2 n is the price $2 and the quantity of insurance services equal to the number of contracts (n), or is the price $100 and the quantity (n/50) or is some other combination relevant? This is an important issue because output quantity figures are needed to investigate the properties of the production of insurance services such as economies of scale and scope and total factor productivity growth.

Insurance firms are financial intermediaries whose outputs are contingent claims. That is, the claim is paid contingent upon the occurrence of the insured event or events. These contingent claims represent the financial protection through risk pooling provided to individuals. There are many characteristics associated with the contingent claims as each contract can represent a different contingent claim. In the insurance industry the latter is referred to as a policy.

There are four basic characteristics of an insurance policy. The first characteristic represents the insured event, which for example can relate to life, property, health or unemployment. Second is the surrender value which relates to the amount available in cash upon voluntary termination of a policy before it becomes payable by death or maturity. The surrender value distinguishes term from basic insurance—for the former there is no surrender value. The third characteristic is the face value of the policy. This pertains to the value received by the insured if the event that is being insured against occurs. The last basic characteristic pertains to the policyholder, either an individual or group and the group can consist of various numbers of individuals. There are many other characteristics or riders of an insurance policy such as double indemnity which is a benefit in a life insurance policy providing for the payment of an additional amount equal to the face value of the policy in case of death by accident. Another rider is the disability waiver which is a benefit such that if the insurer is unable to pay the premium due to a disability, then the insurance firm will waive the premium while keeping the policy in force.

The outputs of the insurance firm are characterized by the number of policies classified according to the various characteristics or riders. Each bundle of characteristics represents a policy and the number of policies with identical characteristics represents the quantity of a particular output of the insurance firm. Returning to our simple example where n is the number of contracts of the single type of policy, n is the output quantity since n represents the number of contingent claims for a particular policy, and $2 is the price.

Standard Industrial Classification

Under the standard industrial classification (SIC), insurance output is more or less categorized by the insured event so that within major group 73, which is insurance industries, there are the subgroups life insurers (731), deposit insurers (732), and property and casualty insurers (733). As part of the contingent claims offered by insurance firms, individuals are able to accumulate financial assets. This fact is reflected in life insurance policies and annuities which are classified within group 731. However, there are policies which are not subject to the investment restrictions on the insurers' portfolio set out in the insurance act. These policies are classified in the group called segregated funds, which is SIC 7213. Segregated funds are in the group of portfolio intermediaries which is 721 and the latter is in major group 72, which is investment intermediary industries.

In this study we consider the groups 7311, life insurers; 7331, health insurers (we do not include government health insurance); 7339, other property and casualty insurers (we do not include unemployment insurance and workmen's compensation); and the last group is 7213, segregated funds. The outputs of insurance firms are usually aggregated into two groups, life insurance (7311 and 7213) and property and casualty insurance (7331 and 7339).

Life Insurance Output

Life insurance output can be further classified according to the other basic characteristics: surrender value, face value and policyholders (individual versus group). Table 16 provides a breakdown of the various outputs under the life insurance category. There are 17 output categories listed in table 16.

Table 16
Output Categories and Unit Costs of Life Insurance Firms

Output Categories	Unit Cost*
Ordinary Insurance	
First year	$100.00 per policy
Term and temporary additions	$ 10.92 per $1,000 new effected
Basic insurance	$ 28.22 per $1,000 new effected
Renewal	$ 7.10 per policy
Term and temporary additions	$ 0.94 per $1,000 in force
Basic insurance	$ 2.03 per $1,000 in force
Group Insurance	
First year	$100.00 per policy
	$ 1.35 per $1,000 new effected
Renewal	$ 0.65 per $1,000 in force
Ordinary Deferred Annuities	
First year	$100.00 per policy
	$ 31.25 per $1,000 annual payment, new effected; 80$ of first year premium income
Renewal	$ 6.60 per policy
	$ 1.67 per $1,000 annual payment, in force; 4.5$ of renewal premium income
Single premium annuities	5.0 percent of single premium income (net of dividends to policyholders)
Group Annuities	
First year	$100.00 per policy
	20 percent of premium income
Renewal	10 percent of renewal premium income
Single premium	3 percent of single premium income (net of dividends to policyholders)
Vested Annuities (ordinary and group)	$ 12.00 per policy
Mortgage and Real Estate Assets	0.32 percent of assets ($)
Policy Loans	0.64 percent of assets ($)
Segregated Funds	0.18 percent of assets ($)
Balance of Ledger Assets	0.12 percent of assets ($)

Note: *The unit costs are derived from the report of the Expense Committee of the Canadian Institute of Actuaries, 1971, and modified as described in Hirshhorn and Geehan 1977.

Notice that new policies and renewals are distinguished since the former require considerably greater selling effort. In general, in terms of the services provided by the industry, renewals constitute a distinct product. A distinction is also made between term and basic ordinary insurance. This separation is important because term and temporary insurance have been increasing much faster than basic insurance over the last two and a half decades.

While table 16 reflects the multiplicity of services produced by life insurance firms, there has still been an aggregation of services into "product lines." Each of these product lines, however, is defined by policies which have common characteristics. Aggregation is inevitable in any empirical analysis because of the practical difficulty of taking explicit account of the entire spectrum of policies as separate outputs. Issues of aggregation, however, are quite distinct from the characterization of the outputs in the insurance industry.

Output aggregation is also necessary when productivity growth (whether partial or total) in the industry is to be measured. To aggregate the various outputs into a single index, their prices and quantities are needed. Quantities are the number of contracts or constant dollars in each of the categories in table 16, while instead of prices, unit costs are used as the weights to form the aggregate output index. Under the assumptions of constant returns to scale and output price-taking behaviour on the part of the insurance firms (i.e., the insurance industry is purely competitive with respect to each of its products), product prices are equated to marginal costs which, in turn, are equated to average or unit costs. Hence, under these assumptions it is appropriate to use unit costs as the weights in forming an aggregate output index. Indeed, profits do not account for more than 2 percent of operating expenses over the period 1961 to 1985.

Unit costs used as weights in the aggregate output index are presented in table 16. The unit costs were derived from the formula used by the Canadian Institute of Actuaries (1971). A Laspeyres quantity index of output was then computed. The index is presented in table 17. The aggregation of output by using 17 different output categories captures, to a certain extent, the introduction of new products (i.e., new policies) and the changing significance in terms of revenue generation of existing products. For example, we have tried to capture the growth in importance of variable policies by treating "segregated funds" as a distinct category. However, given the data, it is impossible to consider all the changes which have taken place in the insurance industry's outputs. For example, there are no data which could allow us to account for new intermediation services which are ancillary to life insurance, such as estate planning and tax advice. While it would be more desirable to allow for these changes, given the relatively minor revenue share of these

Table 17
Life Insurance Output Indices

Year	Index of Output	Index of Output per Employee
1961	100.0	100.0
1962	101.8	99.8
1963	107.8	103.7
1964	113.3	106.7
1965	118.0	110.3
1966	121.4	110.1
1967	125.9	109.5
1968	131.8	115.7
1969	129.9	111.6
1970	135.1	114.3
1971	146.1	124.9
1972	154.7	132.3
1973	165.0	137.6
1974	171.3	142.6
1975	180.0	143.9
1976	195.4	160.6
1977	205.9	169.3
1978	204.4	163.0
1979	215.4	164.0
1980	230.7	170.5
1981	265.0	176.7
1982	295.0	195.7
1983	316.9	214.8
1984	343.2	232.7
1985	389.9	253.6
Average Annual Growth Rate		
	5.83 percent	3.95 percent

Source: Authors' estimates.

services, their inclusion in the aggregate output index would not significantly influence the measure.

From table 17, the aggregate output index which was 100 in 1961 grew to almost 390 in 1985. Thus, the average annual growth rate was 5.83 percent, which compares to 4.08 percent in the manufacturing industries and 4.39 percent for the economy as a whole. Also found in table 17 is the index of output per employee which was also based in 1961 and grew to almost 254 in 1985. This partial productivity index relating to labour shows that labour productivity grew at the average annual rate of 3.95 percent. This figure compares to 3.08 percent in the manufacturing industries and 2.77 percent for the economy as a whole.

Property/Casualty Insurance Output

For property and casualty insurance, there are three services which are identified; property, automobile and other casualty. The aggregate output index is calculated in the same manner as for life insurance, i.e., as a Laspeyres quantity index. Base year weights for each service category are calculated as net premiums earned minus claims paid plus imputed interest. These weights are used to aggregate the three output indices which are formed from deflated values of premiums earned for each category. The deflator for property is a weighted average of homeowners' and tenants' insurance components of the consumer price index (CPI); the weights are obtained from the Survey of Consumer Expenditure. The deflator for automobile is the automobile insurance component of the CPI. The last deflator for other casualty is the average price index of the previous two deflators. Imputed interest is calculated as the ratio of liabilities to policyholders to total liabilities, with the ratio multiplied by total investment income. Imputed interest is deflated by the CPI.

The three services categories are aggregated as a Laspeyres quantity index by using the base year weights. Table 18 shows the aggregate output index for property and casualty insurance. The index grows from a base of 100.0 in 1961 to 192.8 in 1985 which implies an average annual growth rate of 2.77 percent, about half the growth rate for life insurance. In addition, labour productivity for property and casualty shows virtually no change between 1975 and 1985, although the index increased up to 1978 and then declined until 1982. From 1979 to 1983 firms supplying property and casualty insurance faced underwriting losses, although these were more than fully covered by the high earnings on financial investments. Data on employment in casualty and property are only available for the period after 1974 from the Insurance Bureau of Canada. The employment data from this source for the

Table 18
Property and Casualty Insurance Output Indices

Year	Index of Output	Index of Output per Employee
1961	100.0	
1962	104.3	
1963	108.6	
1964	109.9	
1965	109.8	
1966	111.5	
1967	118.7	
1968	125.9	
1969	131.8	
1970	136.7	
1971	141.3	
1972	144.8	
1973	147.2	
1974	161.3	
1975	157.9	100.0
1976	162.8	103.4
1977	179.5	112.8
1978	189.7	118.0
1979	193.1	114.4
1980	199.2	112.5
1981	182.8	94.2
1982	175.3	88.2
1983	179.2	90.9
1984	184.0	95.3
1985	192.8	98.8
Average Annual Growth Rate		
	2.77 percent	0.00 percent

Source: Authors' estimates.

private sector firms are complemented by data for provincial government insurance corporations from annual reports.

The combined results for life and property/casualty insurance are reported in table 19. Output for the insurance industry grew at an annual average rate of 4.38 percent over the period 1961-85, while the index of output per employee grew at the rate of 3.07 percent.

Table 19

Combined Results of Life and Property and Casualty Insurance

Year	Index of Output	Index of Output per Employee
1961	100.0	100.0
1962	103.2	101.1
1963	108.2	103.1
1964	111.4	103.7
1965	113.4	103.5
1966	115.9	103.5
1967	121.9	102.3
1968	128.5	105.1
1969	130.9	105.0
1970	136.0	107.4
1971	143.4	113.0
1972	149.2	122.8
1973	155.1	133.0
1974	165.7	139.2
1975	167.7	139.0
1976	177.2	142.3
1977	191.2	142.5
1978	196.2	146.3
1979	202.9	149.0
1980	213.1	156.7
1981	219.2	154.9
1982	228.3	153.4
1983	240.1	168.4
1984	254.5	184.8
1985	280.0	206.5
Average Annual Growth Rate		
	4.38 percent	3.07 percent

Source: Authors' estimates.

Before completing this section on output measurement, we should explain in more detail the reasons behind the imputation of interest in the determination of the aggregate output index in property/casualty insurance. We argued that premiums minus claims (net of any re-insurance) is the appropriate measure of revenues for insurance firms since it reflects the earnings from risk pooling or providing contingent claims. However, the bulk (about 60 percent) of investment earnings for property/casualty firms are derived from funds which are, in effect, loaned by policyholders. These funds appear as liabilities on the balance sheet and are recorded under "unearned premiums," "provision for unpaid claims," and "other policy reserves." No explicit interest is paid on the liabilities. For example, the provision for unpaid claims remains a liability for the period between the time the claim is first incurred and the time it is paid. In addition, premiums are paid in advance of or at the beginning of the period covered by a policy. If the period of the policy is one year, after four months one-third of the premium is taken into revenue as earned, the other two-thirds remains as the liability "unearned premiums." Thus, property/casualty firms are able to offer contingent claims or policies at a lower premium because premiums are paid in advance of claims and in advance of the time period to be covered by the policy, and these funds earn a positive rate of return. This return must be added to the premiums minus claims magnitude in order to obtain the total revenue attributable to property/casualty insurance provision.

At the present time in the Canadian system of national accounts and in the United Nations system of national accounts, revenue attributable to property/casualty insurance is computed as premiums minus claims. Thus, when all costs of insurance provision are subtracted from revenues the so-called underwriting gain is usually negative. Our proposal parallels the argument for imputed interest in the banking industry. After adding the interest imputation, property/casualty insurance would be treated in the way which is conceptually correct and similar to banks. The underwriting gain, which includes imputed interest, now becomes positive for 24 of the past 25 years.

INPUT MEASUREMENT

The major inputs used to provide insurance services are labour, materials and capital. Labour costs are generally calculated as the sum of commissions, wages, salaries and allowances plus employees' and agents' supplementary income benefits. Labour cost is presented in the first column of table 20. We calculate that labour cost grew by an average annual rate of about 10 percent. The quantity of labour input is derived by dividing labour cost by the average hourly earnings. This procedure leads to the labour input index presented in the second column of table 20. The labour input index grew at an average an-

Table 20
Labour and Material and Capital Input Index and Cost for Life and Property and Casualty Insurance

Year	Labour Cost ($000,000)	Labour Input Index	Material and Capital Cost ($000,000)	Material and Capital Input Index
1961	311	100	300	100
1962	322	99	312	102
1963	346	104	323	104
1964	374	107	350	107
1965	402	107	397	109
1966	443	113	410	107
1967	483	115	459	117
1968	534	122	501	125
1969	580	125	566	136
1970	626	126	631	143
1971	679	126	755	161
1972	734	124	849	173
1973	819	124	964	185
1974	998	136	1120	201
1975	1123	140	1267	198
1976	1312	150	1551	216
1977	1391	147	1833	237
1978	1583	152	1886	235
1979	1809	158	2054	252
1980	2035	161	2290	275
1981	2285	163	2642	301
1982	2684	172	3186	313
1983	2887	170	3443	311
1984	3053	165	4163	343
Average Annual Growth Rate				
	9.98 percent	2.20 percent	11.16 percent	5.27 percent

Source: Authors' estimates.

nual rate of 2.2 percent. This implies that the average hourly earnings for labour grew by more than three times the growth rate in the quantity of labour.

Materials and capital are the other two factors in the production process. It is important to note that for property/casualty insurance materials include commissions (a service input) paid to independent agents who are the most significant sellers of this type of insurance. The third column of table 20 shows material/capital cost which grew at an average annual rate of just over 11 percent. Using the price index for material/capital input, the input index is calculated and presented in the last column. This index grew at an average annual rate of around 5.3 percent. Material/capital inputs grew at more than twice the rate of labour inputs, while the price of the former factor of production grew by more than twice its input index.

ECONOMIES OF SCALE AND SCOPE

The vast majority of studies focus on the relationship between average costs and aggregate output and thereby attempt to estimate economies of scale. Economies of scope relate to the economies from product diversity as opposed to product specialization. Economies of scope exist if the cost of producing many products together (e.g., in one plant) is less than the cost of producing the products separately (e.g., in different plants). Economies of scope are clearly illustrated by railroads producing both passenger and freight services using the same rail bed. As another example, taxi firms clearly enjoy economies of scope in the provision of two products—trips to the airport, trips from the airport—yet many cities allow all firms to sell the first product but bar some firms from selling *both* services. In life insurance, economies of scope may result from the cost savings associated with the sales efforts of an agent who can provide a variety of term, whole life and annuity policies. Economies of scope may result from joint production of property/liability and life insurance products, or from joint production of insurance, deposit, and securities brokerage services.

If costs grow in a greater (lesser) proportion to output growth, there are scale economies (diseconomies). These phenomena are also referred to as increasing and decreasing returns to scale. If costs and output grow at the same rate, returns to scale are constant. Most studies have defined output in terms of premiums or claims. We have argued that this definition is incorrect, not just because of aggregation problems arising from product heterogeneity and price differentials, but rather because of the characteristics supplied by insurance firms which relate to contingent claims. Premiums (whether or not they are deflated) do not capture the risk pooling nature of insurance. Most researchers recognize the deficiencies of using premiums as the output variable. Geehan (1977) has shown that there is an upward bias in estimates of scale economies when premiums are the output indicators.

Two different model structures have been used to attempt to avoid the limitations of premiums as an output measure. The first approach is to estimate separate cost functions for different output categories with premiums for the specific output class used as the indicator (see Halpern and Mathewson 1975). The second approach is to introduce additional variables which reflect product heterogeneity such as the ratio of group life to total life, average policy size, and surrender ratio, to name just a few of the variables (see Praetz 1980). These two approaches attempt to deal with the aggregation problem associated with the multiplicity of outputs but do not solve the inherent problems of using premiums as the output variable. In these studies, costs are defined to include commissions, wages and salaries, rent, depreciation, materials, purchased services and supplies.

The studies summarized in table 21 provide evidence on the existence of scale economies. A number of conclusions emerge from the results in table 21. First, there is virtually no evidence of diseconomies of scale. Secondly, there may be economies of scale, but these economies are found for relatively small output quantities. Thus, firms in the U.S., Canada, U.K. and Australia generally produce where returns to scale are constant. Some studies which do find rather large scale economies for wide output ranges may have biased estimates because of their inappropriate output measures. The third result is that there is a high degree of residual variation in the average cost across firms which is not accounted for by product mix and output. This may be the result of limited information on the part of consumers which permits high unit cost and thereby allows high price firms to survive along with low price firms.

There is only one study which has looked at the evidence regarding economies of scope or product diversity. Kellner and Mathewson (1983) investigate scale and scope economies for the Canadian life insurance industry. The outputs were measured as the number of contracts in force. Four outputs were distinguished: individual ordinary life insurance policies, group life insurance policies, individual ordinary annuities, and group annuities. Revenues were also measured as premiums minus claims minus re-insurance. Kellner and Mathewson estimated that for the years 1961, 1966 and 1971 scale economies could be rejected but there was some slight evidence of scale economies in 1976. For the four years the scale elasticities were .98, .83, .83, and 1.09.

With respect to scope economies, there was evidence of their existence for the years 1961, 1966 and 1971 between ordinary life (both individual and group) and annuity outputs. There was evidence of scope economies between

Table 21

Summary of Studies of Economies of Scale in Insurance

Author(s)	*Country/Industry*	*Output or Scale*	*Other Expanatory Variables*	*Special Features*	*Conclusions*
D.W. Colenutt	United Kingdom ordinary life	Premiums	Ratios of single premiums, immediate annuity considerations, annuity contracts, new yearly business, group business, lapses and surrenders, overseas business; average policy size; stock vs. mutual; emphasis on policies for investment	Companies with less than £250,000 premiums are excluded from the sample of 49 companies	Increasing returns to scale; MES = £20 million of premiums approximately
R. Geehan	Canada life	Weighted sum of activities	Age of firm, stock vs. mutual, a measure of deviation from capacity output	Separate regressions for head office activities, investment activities, all activities combined including and excluding tax costs	Increasing returns to scale, strongest for head office output; MES = $2 million of output ($5 million premiums)

T.V. Daula	United States life	Weighted sum of activities	Stock vs. mutual, age of company, subsidiary of larger company vs. independent	Sixty companies in sample	Increasing returns to scale
P. Praetz (1980)	United States life	Premiums net of reinsurance	Proportions of new business, policies lapsed, group business, health business, industrial business, whole life and endowment, average policy size	Sample of 90 selected to improve homogeneity	Increasing returns to scale; some evidence of U-shaped LAC
P. Praetz (1981)	Australia life	Premiums	Proportions of new business and whole life	Separate and combined regressions for superannuation business and ordinary life	Increasing returns to scale, especially for superannuation business
R.J. Hensley	United States property liability	Premiums	This is not a regression study; expense ratios are calculated for each of four size groups (three for mutuals)	Firm data are averaged over five years; separate calculations for stock vs. mutual	Increasing returns to scale for both stock and mutual companies

Author(s)	*Country/Industry*	*Output or Scale*	*Other Expanatory Variables*	*Special Features*	*Conclusions*
J.D. Cummins	United States independent insurance agencies	(1) Premiums (2) Number of accounts	Average size of account, measures of life and health business, commercial vs. personal accounts, direct billing, policyowner income (a proxy for service level), urban center vs. other (proxy for factor price differences)	Separate and combined regressions for three size groups; long run and short run cost functions are estimated separately	Constant returns to scale in long run
J. Johnston, G.W. Murphey	United Kingdom life	Premiums	New premiums as a percentage of total premiums; the expense ratio (operating costs/premiums) is adjusted for single premiums	Separate analyses for composite, industrial-ordinary, specialist life offices; separate analyses of companies grouped by degree of schemes (group) business	Increasing returns to scale
S.T. Pritchett (1971)	United States ordinary life	Weighted sum of activities ("standard expense")	This is not a regression analysis; the ratio of actual to standard expense is calculated; the average ratio for each of 4 size groups is compared	Data are averaged for three years; the sample size was 30	Increasing returns to scale

S.T. Pritchett (1973)	United States ordinary life	Weighted sum of activities	Similar in design to Pritchett (1971)	Emphasis is on analysing the behavior of costs over time, by size group; separate analysis of home office vs. field expense; the sample size was 30	Average costs first fall with increasing scale then rise for largest group
S.T. Pritchett (1974)	United States ordinary life	Weighted sum of activities	Same cost data as Pritchett (1971)	Data points are fitted to a non-linear regression line; price-scale relation is investigated	Increasing returns to scale; price-scale relation may be U-shaped
D.B. Houston, R.M. Simon	United States life	Premiums	Proportions of industrial, group, new premiums; lapse plus surrender ratio; mutual vs. stock company	Large sample, 237 companies	Increasing returns; MES = \$100 million of premiums
D.J.S. Rutledge, R.H. Tuckwell	Australia life	Premiums	Proportions of new business, policies surrendered, policies forfeited, superannuation business; average size of policies	Separate and combined regressions for ordinary and superannuation business; 5 small and/or new firms excluded from sample of 41	Constant returns to scale

Author(s)	*Country/Industry*	*Output or Scale*	*Other Expanatory Variables*	*Special Features*	*Conclusions*
P.L. Joskow	United States property-liability	Direct premiums	Separate cost and scale variables for direct writers vs. agency companies; ratio of net to direct premiums (accounts for reinsurance activity)	Separate regressions for: stock auto, mutual auto, stock fire	Constant returns to scale; lower costs for direct vs. agency
P.J. Halpern, G.F. Mathewson	Canadian general	Net premiums written	Proxies for service quality, claim settlement procedures, loss ratio, diversification, opportunity cost of financial capital	Model assumes marginal cost is equated to marginal revenue, each specified as a linear function of explanatory variables; separate regressions by line and by stock vs. mutual	Constant returns for stock companies; evidence supports economies of scale for mutual companies
R.D. Blair, J.R. Jackson, R.J. Vogel	United States health	Premiums written	Ratio of group premiums to total, degree of specialization in health insurance, company type (e.g., health specialty, life and health), stock vs. mutual	Model is adapted from Houston and Simon; authors note that average size of group policy may be important but data are lacking for test	Increasing returns to scale; costs are higher for stock vs. mutual companies

S.T. Pritchett, J.E. Logan	United States worker's compensation	(1) Premiums earned, worker's compensation (2) Premiums earned, all lines	This is not a regression analysis; firms are grouped by size with expense ratios reported as group means, ranges, etc.	Expense ratios are reported by type: adjustment, commissions and broker's fees, other acquisition, general, other; acquisition expense is main source of scale effects; sample consists of 53 mutual companies	Increasing returns to scale using worker's compensation premiums; uncertain results for premiums, all lines
J.D. Hammond, E.R. Mellander, N. Shilling	United States property liability	Net premiums	Agency system (independent vs. exclusive), stock vs. mutual, premium mix, capacity measure (premiums less or more than policy-holder surplus)	Separate regressions for (1) loss adjustment expenses, (2) direct commissions, (3) total underwriting expenses, (4) operating expenses ((1) plus (3)), (5) losses (claims) plus (1)	Increasing returns for each type of cost except (5); MES = $385 million for operating expenses (4)
R.F. Allen	United States stock property liability	Scale or capacity, policyholders' surplus; actual output, net premiums	Capacity utilization (premiums/policyholders' surplus), loss/premium ratio	Sample is selected for comparable premium mix, pricing policy, distribution system; separate and combined regressions for 3 size groups	Increasing returns to scale for smallest size group only; MES = $30 to $60 million of net premiums

individual and group outputs for both ordinary life and annuities. In addition, for the years with evidence of scale economies, there was no evidence of scope economies.

An important area for future research is to develop and empirically implement models to investigate scale and scope economies for property/casualty insurance and for life and property/casualty insurance combined.

FACTOR SUBSTITUTION AND PRODUCTIVITY GROWTH

Few studies have investigated the extent to which factors are substitutable and the rate of productivity growth in the provision of insurance services. One study has looked at factor substitution in the Canadian life insurance industry. Daly, Rao and Geehan (1985) estimated that all factors respond to their own prices, with inelastic (i.e., between 0 and -1) price effects. The factors of production in their model were labour (which includes commissions because most life insurance salesmen are company employees), capital (buildings) and materials (which was an aggregation of legal, medical, advertising and accounting and other expenses). The inputs were estimated to be substitutes for each other; an increase in the price of one input caused an increase in the demand for the other factors. Hence, as factor prices increased, insurance firms substituted the relatively cheaper inputs into the production process. These cross price effects were quite small. Table 22 shows the price effects obtained by Daly, Rao and Geehan (1985). There is no evidence in the literature on the factor price effects for property/casualty insurance firms.

Table 22
Factor Price Elasticities

Factor Demand	Factor Price	Elasticity* (percent)
Capital	Capital	–0.656
Labour	Labour	–0.165
Materials	Materials	–0.677
Capital	Labour	0.035
Capital	Materials	0.298
Labour	Materials	0.134

Source: Daly, Rao and Geehan 1985.

Note: *Based on a 1 percent increase in the price.

Table 23
Sources and Average Annual Rates of Output Growth

	1961–66	1967–73	1974–77	1978–84
Labour	1.48	0.80	2.61	1.00
Materials/Capital	0.54	3.25	2.56	2.17
Productivity	0.96	0.19	0.21	1.00
Output	2.98	4.24	5.38	4.17

Source: Authors' estimates.

Estimates of (total factor) productivity growth are found in two studies. For the Canadian life insurance industry, Daly, Rao and Geehan (1985) estimated that annual productivity growth was 1.1 percent from 1962 to 1966, 2.1 percent from 1967 to 1973, and 2.4 percent from 1974 to 1977. These productivity growth rates exceeded the rate of 0.95 percent which was estimated for Canadian manufacturing over the period 1946-76 (see May and Denny 1979).

The sources of productivity growth in the Canadian life insurance industry are dominated by technological change and unexplained residual effects due to the possibility of lags in the adjustment of labour and capital in the production process and product demand shifts. Over the period 1962 to 1977, technological change accounted for around 65 percent of productivity growth.

Weiss (1986) measured productivity growth for the U.S. life insurance industry. She found that for stock insurance firms annual productivity growth for the period 1976 to 1980 was 0.95 percent and for mutual firms for the period 1975 to 1979 the growth rate was about 1.03 percent.

Total factor productivity growth can be measured when data on output and inputs are available. Using our output index (table 19) along with the labour and material/capital input indices (table 20), the average annual rates of productivity growth in Canada for life and property/casualty insurance are presented in table 23, calculated as the difference between the growth rate of output and the weighted growth rates of inputs. The weights represent the contribution of input costs to total costs and are calculated here using fixed weights of 60/40 for labour and materials/capital. The third row in the table shows that productivity growth was around 1 percent per year except for the period in the late '60s to late '70s. During this time there was virtually no growth in productivity. The lack of productivity growth during this period was attributable to property/casualty insurance, since productivity growth for life insurance was over 2 percent. Indeed, over the whole period productivity growth in life insurance exceeded the rate for property/casualty. From 1967 to 1973, output growth for property/casualty was on average only 3.65 percent per year (see table 18). Since labour and material/capital inputs for both types of insurance grew at roughly the same rates, the relatively poor output performance of property/casualty insurance was due to the low growth in productivity.

Clearly, there is a need for much more evidence on the structure of production for life and property/casualty insurance services. Indeed, other than estimating measures of scale economies (although incorrect output measures were generally used) little has been done, and there is virtually no evidence on the issues of scope economies and productivity growth.

CONCLUSIONS

Although more research is needed regarding the structure of production of insurance services, some tentative policy conclusions can be drawn. First, it appears that the provision of life insurance does not constitute a natural monopoly. There do not seem to be significant scale economies, nor do scope economies appear to be pervasive in the industry. Secondly, there is evidence that any scale economies in life and property/casualty insurance exist for only very small levels of output. Thus, the industry is characterized by a large number of firms with a significant diversity of sizes.

The third conclusion is that entry is relatively easy or costless in the insurance industry. There are no entry barriers, and prices appear to equal average costs so there is little, if any, monopoly profit. However, there are substantial differences in prices among insurance firms for similar policies. To the extent that this diversity exists, it may be the result of greater variation in product quality or greater informational asymmetries on the part of consumers than has hitherto been empirically investigated.

Finally, we note that productivity growth in the life insurance industry has been strong and indeed above that for manufacturing industries. On the other hand, productivity has been virtually flat for the property/casualty industry. This result implies that technological change has been more important in life insurance production compared to the provision of property/casualty insurance.

Chapter 5

Insurance Companies As Financial Intermediaries

LIFE INSURANCE COMPANIES

Life insurance companies obtain funds through the sale, usually on an instalment basis, of contingent claims to annuitants and policyholders. The timing and amount of payment on these claims is contingent on the events (death, disability, number of years of survival of a pension beneficiary) which form the conditions of the contract. The value of these claims is recorded as reserve liabilities of the insurance companies and, in the Financial Flow Accounts of the Canadian System of National Accounts, as assets of persons.

The gross inflows of funds from insurance premiums, annuity considerations (payments made to purchase annuities) and investment income *less* gross outflows of claims, annuity benefits and operating expenses *equals* the net internally generated source of funds. These internally generated funds are used to lend to other sectors of the economy via the acquisition of financial assets. In this way, part of life insurance premiums constitute personal savings and are channelled by life companies to help finance real capital formation. Since debt is a negligible item on the balance sheet of the industry, borrowing is not a significant source of funds to the industry, nor is debt retirement a significant use of funds.

In 1985, about 35 percent of gross inflows of funds were from annuity considerations, about 25 percent from life insurance premiums and 40 percent from investment income. In turn, about 12.5 percent of this gross inflow was used to pay operating expenses and taxes, 44 percent was paid out in current claims and benefits, 0.2 percent to shareholders and the remaining 43.3 percent was used to acquire assets. The fraction of each dollar received on a given type of policy which is retained for the acquisition of assets depends on the operating expenses associated with the particular product (individual term contracts are more expensive to service than group life contracts) and on the average deferral period before claims or benefits are paid.

Factors Affecting the Flow of Funds

A larger fraction of a dollar of whole life insurance premiums (compared to term premiums) is retained for the acquisition of assets because whole life, especially in the policy's early years, contains a significant savings component. Similarly, a dollar of deferred annuity premiums goes almost entirely to acquire assets which may be held for many years before liquidation, but a single premium annuity pays benefits immediately, leaving a somewhat smaller fraction to be invested for payment of future benefits. In this way, the product mix of the industry influences its growth as a financial intermediary. No aggregate data exist to show precisely the net internally generated flow of funds by product line, but we do know that both whole life and annuities generate more than term or group life per dollar of premiums. Hence, a number of general trends can usefully be analysed as factors contributing to the growth rate of the industry as a financial institution.

Individual insurance premiums (whole life and term) constitute a decreasing fraction of total premium and annuity income of the industry, falling from nearly 70 percent in 1961 to less than 30 percent in 1985. Furthermore, individual term insurance has risen relative to individual whole life at the same time as group (term) insurance has risen relative to individual insurance.

Since we have incomplete data on premium income of individual term insurance—term insurance is often sold in combination with whole life but published data refer to pure term contracts only—the relative growth of the three components of life insurance is measured as face amounts (gross sales). Individual whole life insurance in 1961 constituted over 40 percent of the total of individual whole life plus individual term plus group life, whereas by 1985 this proportion had fallen to less than 33 percent. In the most recent five years or so, the trend toward a decreasing share of sales for individual whole life has been reversed as a result of the popularity of new products. In particular, these are "new money policies," in which the premiums are revised periodically to reflect current and expected interest rates, and "universal life" policies, in which premiums (less expense charges) are credited to a policy account from which periodic charges for life insurance coverage are deducted and to which interest is credited. Usually, the policyholder can vary the amount and timing of premium payments and change the amount of insurance. In effect, with a universal life policy, one has the flexibility of "buying term and investing the rest," with the investment remaining in the company. The introduction of universal life policies created a virtual revolution in the U.S. in the late '70s and in the '80s. They have proven to be less popular in Canada, but by 1985 they constituted 12 percent of the face value of all individual life insurance purchases. Universal life policies were introduced in Canada in 1981 but were slow to become popular partly because of the uncertainty of their tax treatment.

The evidence to this point establishes the long-term trend away from the traditional main product of life insurance companies, namely whole life, and toward term insurance, both group and individual. These trends were moderated and perhaps reversed in the '80s. The long-term trend had been unfavourable to the growth of life company assets.

Annuities

Relative to all types of life insurance, annuities have grown very rapidly, especially during the '70s. Individual annuity income grew from about 5 percent of total insurance premiums and annuity considerations to 10 percent in 1971 to a peak of 35 percent in 1981 and levelled off to 30 percent in 1985. Group annuity considerations (life company managed pension funds) fluctuated only moderately throughout the '60s in a range of 16 to 21 percent of total life premium plus annuity income, then climbed in the '70s and '80s to reach 30 percent in 1985.

The growth of individual annuities is a story worth recounting as it illustrates the impact of tax rules on product growth. In 1957, registered retirement savings plans (RRSPs) were introduced under federal government legislation. They permitted individuals to defer taxes on part of their income, namely on contributions to and investment earnings within an RRSP. The contributions and the compounded investment income earned on accumulated contributions remain untaxed until the RRSP is collapsed, perhaps as late as age 71. The rules governing RRSPs were made more flexible and the maximum contributions were increased over the years, with major changes in 1972 and 1975, while at the same time effective average marginal tax rates rose, making RRSPs more attractive.

From 1957 to 1972 new registrations grew slowly, and the life insurance industry's share increased from 24 percent in 1957 to over 50 percent by 1970. After this, new registrations grew explosively from 186,000 in 1971 to over 2 million in 1985. However, the share of life companies fell to 15 percent by 1985, as new competitors, chiefly the chartered banks, took over the market. By 1985, chartered banks' share had increased to rival that of the traditional leader, namely trust and mortgage loan companies.

Both annuities and life insurance policies can be registered, but most life companies' RRSPs are individual annuities. In addition to RRSP annuities, life companies benefitted during the 1970s from tax rules permitting non-registered income averaging annuities. In the 1981 budget, income averaging annuities were eliminated and increased taxes were imposed on non-registered contracts. These measures were a substantial blow to the growth of individual annuities.

RRSPs were an obvious benefit to the growth of the life insurance industry, but their growth has also had less obvious effects. RRSPs are a substitute, however imperfect, for the savings component of life insurance policies because acquisition of the latter is partly motivated by the desire to provide for retirement years. If life companies had captured most of the RRSP money, they would have suffered no loss owing to substitution from life policies to RRSPs, but they did not get most of the RRSP business. On the other hand, RRSPs managed by any financial institution (or, indeed, self-directed RRSPs) must be collapsed by age 71 or converted to an annuity or a RRIF (registered retirement investment fund). RRIFs have proven to be less popular than annuities, and since only life companies can offer annuities, they have benefited from RRSPs even when the RRSP is registered with a bank, trust company or credit union.

We conclude the discussion of changes in product mix and its effect on asset accumulation by noting that in 1985 life companies' annuity reserves were 76 percent of total reserves, with life insurance reserves making up the remaining 24 percent. This is a reversal of the pattern of the 1960s. In 1970, annuity reserves were only 35 percent of the total; life insurance reserves were 65 percent of the total.

Asset Growth

On balance, the changes in product mix and the overall growth rate of the industry were unfavourable for asset growth relative to most other financial institutions and relative to total financial assets held by all sectors of the economy.

Table 24 shows that life insurance companies over the 25-year period 1961-85 lost position relative to every major financial sector: banks, trust and mortgage loan, credit unions, trusteed pension plans and even property and casualty insurance companies. According to data in Neufeld (1972:254), this decline in the relative size of life companies has been going on since at least the 1940s. From 1981 to 1985 the downward trend appears to have been reversed, in part because of the slowdown in chartered banks' growth.

Table 25 shows the claims of the personal sector on life companies as a proportion of total personal sector financial assets. These data confirm the relative decline of life companies from 1961-81 followed by a trend reversal for 1981-85 and continuing into 1986. These same trends are further confirmed in the first row of table 27 which shows the proportion of financial assets by all sectors of the economy which are held by life companies.

Table 24

Financial Assets of Major Financial Institutions

(billions of dollars and percentage of total)

	1961	1966	1971	1976	1981	1985
Chartered Banks	$14.1	$24.3	$44.9	$101.5	$236.4	$293.9
	44.2%	44.3%	48.2%	50.0%	52.0%	44.5%
Credit Unions and	$ 1.4	$ 2.8	$ 5.4	$ 15.5	$ 33.3	$ 45.7
Caisses Populaires	4.4%	5.1%	5.8%	7.6%	7.3%	6.9%
Trust and Mortgage	$ 2.6	$ 6.4	$11.5	$ 28.7	$ 63.6	$120.0
Loan Companies	8.2%	11.7%	12.3%	14.1%	14.0%	18.2%
Trusteed Pension	$ 4.0	$ 7.2	$12.4	$ 24.7	$ 59.6	$104.7
Plans	12.5%	13.1%	13.3%	12.2%	13.1%	15.9%
Life Insurance	$ 8.5	$12.1	$15.7	$ 25.9	$ 49.5	$ 77.7
	26.6%	22.1%	16.8%	12.8%	10.9%	11.8%
Property and	$ 1.3	$ 2.0	$ 3.3	$ 6.7	$ 11.8	$ 17.8
Casualty Insurance	4.1%	3.6%	3.5%	3.3%	2.6%	2.7%
Total of Above	$31.9	$54.8	$93.2	$203.0	$454.2	$659.8
	100.0%	100.0%	100.0%	100.0%	100.0%	100.0%

Source: National Balance Sheet Accounts, Statistics Canada catalogue 13-214.

Notes: Trust company assets exclude estate, trust and agency funds. Life insurance includes accident and sickness branches and includes segregated funds. The 1985 figure for mortgage loan companies is an estimate.

Table 25

Personal Sector Claims on Life Insurance Companies in Relation to Personal Sector Total Financial Assets

Ratio	1961	1966	1971	1976	1981	1985	1986
Life Insurance/ Total Financial Assets	14.22%	12.99%	11.96%	10.79%	9.94%	10.91%	11.13%
Life Insurance/ Total Life Plus Pension Assets of Persons	62.77%	59.98%	55.47%	52.85%	46.45%	43.02%	42.54%

Source: Financial Flow Accounts, Statistics Canada catalogue 13-002.

The second row in table 25 shows that financial assets held by life insurance companies continued to decline relative to trusteed pension plans throughout 1961-86, with no reversal of trend in the 1980s.

Asset Structure

Financial institutions, as a rule, seek to minimize their exposure to the risk inherent in fluctuating interest rates by matching the terms of their assets to that of their liabilities. In this way the promised rate of return on, for example, a ten-year liability can be more or less guaranteed by the acquisition of a financial asset which at the time of purchase has a promised rate of return over the same ten-year period. Fluctuations in market interest rates in the interim will not affect the initial yield to maturity nor the maturity value of the asset, although the interim market price responds in inverse relationship to market interest rates and the terminal value of reinvested interest receipts is also affected by interim fluctuations in interest rates. (In practice, the appropriate measures are the durations of the assets and liabilities, not simply the terms to maturity. A full technical discussion is not necessary to an understanding of the desirability of matching long-term liabilities with long-term assets.)

Since life insurance and pension liabilities are long term in nature (policies are priced on the basis of long-term projections of interest rates), one would expect life companies to prefer long-term assets. Table 26 reveals just such a pattern. Short-term assets comprising cash and deposits, Canada treasury bills and short-term paper equal no more than 6.69 percent of total financial assets. Long-term instruments in the form of bonds and mortgages and (increasingly) stocks form the bulk of the industry's portfolio. Not shown in table 26, which reports only financial assets, is the increased investment in real estate by the industry which rose from about $0.3 billion in 1961 to $4 billion in 1985; however, real estate assets are only about 5 percent of total assets in Canada. Neave (1981:135) argues that taxation revisions of 1970 favoured direct investment by life companies in real estate chiefly because capital cost allowances provided a tax shelter against now higher corporate tax rates.

The proportion of total financial assets held in the form of bonds fell from a high of 49.74 percent in 1961 to a range of about 36 to 41 percent, within which it has fluctuated for the last 20 years. The proportion of municipal bonds declined over the period. The proportion of provincial bonds has remained remarkably stable since 1976. The proportion of Canada bonds rose substantially (at the expense of the share going to corporate bonds) during the 1980s when the federal deficit rose substantially.

Table 26
Life Insurance Companies' Asset Structure
(asset items as a percentage of total financial assets)

	1961	1966	1971	1976	1981	1985	1986
Short-Term Assets	0.93	0.86	2.12	3.53	6.05	6.69	6.56
Loans to Policyholders	4.37	3.91	5.23	4.98	5.35	3.66	3.27
Mortgages	40.14	47.56	44.68	43.07	37.25	30.62	31.83
Bonds							
Federal	8.10	3.84	3.35	2.99	7.67	13.35	12.07
Provincial	10.37	9.57	8.63	7.63	6.80	7.85	7.56
Municipal	7.75	6.50	4.56	2.53	2.24	2.43	2.31
Corporate & Other	23.25	21.59	20.78	22.79	19.84	17.51	17.61
Total Bonds	49.47	41.50	37.32	35.94	36.55	41.14	39.56
Stocks	2.71	3.77	8.73	9.75	9.56	9.75	10.44
Other Assets	2.38	2.40	1.92	2.73	5.23	8.13	8.35
Total	100.00	100.00	100.00	100.00	100.00	100.00	100.00

Source: Financial Flow Accounts, Statistics Canada.

Government regulations limit the kinds and proportions of assets that life insurance companies can hold by restricting bond and stock investments to instruments issued by companies satisfying stipulated conditions of financial strength and also by restricting the value of a mortgage as a proportion of the property value securing it. Regulatory restrictions on the proportions of total assets that may be held in various forms are, potentially, more relevant to this analysis. In 1965 the maximum permitted proportion of common stocks in a company's asset portfolio was raised to 25 percent from 15 percent. This constraint may have been binding for some companies, but it clearly was not for the industry as a whole, as shown in table 26.

The industry was not constrained by regulation as to the proportion of assets held in bonds nor as to the proportion held in mortgages. We must look to factors other than changes in insurance industry regulatory constraints to explain the changes in the industry asset portfolio shown in table 26. Diverse factors caused changes in the "loans to policyholders," "mortgages" and "stocks" items in table 26.

Policyholder Loans

Loans to policyholders have responded to changes in interest rates. Until recent years (when borrowing rates were tied to current market rates), most whole life policies stipulated a maximum interest rate which could be charged on loans by life companies to policyholders. Usually, the policyholder could borrow an amount up to the cash value of the policy. Since older policies contained a clause stipulating a low maximum interest rate (6 percent on policies written prior to September 1968, for example), a rise in market rates tended to make policy loans an attractive alternative to bank or credit union loans. In fact, when market rates rose sufficiently high, policyholders exploited arbitrage opportunities by borrowing and investment in term deposits or other instruments offering yields higher than their borrowing costs. Figure 2 shows this close relationship between market interest rates and the flow (i.e., new borrowing net of repayments) of policy loans.

Mortgage Assets

The proportion of life company assets held as mortgages was in decline from 1966 to 1985, as shown in table 26. Table 27 reveals that a major decline in the importance of life companies in the total Canadian mortgage market relative to other financial institutions also began after 1966. The decline in importance of life companies in the mortgage markets can be traced in large part to the 1967 Bank Act revisions and to changes in the character of NHA mortgages in 1969. Prior to the 1967 Bank Act revisions, chartered banks were prevented from lending at rates in excess of 6 percent, which made Central Mortgage and Housing Corporation (CMHC) insured mortgage loans (the only kind banks were then permitted to hold) unprofitable whenever market rates exceeded this, as was often the case in the '60s. Banks left the mortgage market to others until 1967, after which they became major participants. In 1967 chartered banks held 3.6 percent of the value of mortgages outstanding in Canada; this proportion rose to 11.1 percent in 1976 and 24.3 percent in 1985.

The second major change affecting the mortgage market was that after 1969, National Housing Act (NHA) residential mortgages were no longer required to have amortization periods equal to their terms (usually 25 years). That is to say, prior to 1969, the period over which the loan was repaid and the term over which the interest rate was specified were both usually 25 years. Such an instrument suited very well the life companies' need for a

Figure 2
Flow of Policy Loans and Market Interest Rates

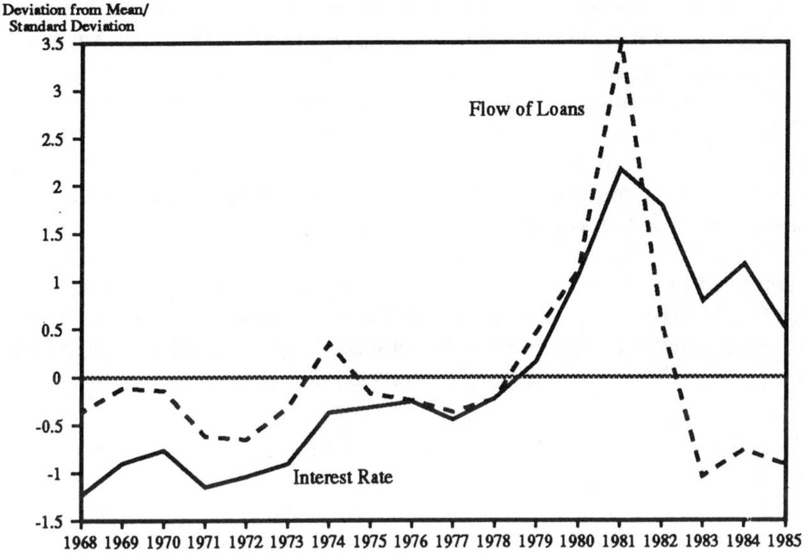

Table 27

Assets of Life Insurance Companies as a Percentage of Total Held by All Sectors of the Economy

	1961	1966	1971	1976	1981	1985	1986
Total Financial Assets	4.74	4.22	3.44	3.01	2.71	3.12	3.72
Mortgages	29.60	27.77	19.09	13.65	12.69	12.97	13.38
Bonds							
Federal	4.11	2.46	2.16	2.26	5.25	7.60	7.11
Provincial	10.77	8.77	5.85	3.95	3.44	4.00	3.97
Municipal	15.58	11.87	7.14	4.30	5.30	7.23	7.63
Corporate & Other	24.44	21.77	17.76	19.53	16.89	17.58	17.01
Total Bonds	54.90	44.86	32.91	30.05	30.88	36.41	35.72
Stocks	1.02	1.16	2.80	3.13	2.76	3.05	3.21

Source: Financial Flow Accounts, Statistics Canada.

long-term asset to match to its long-term liabilities, but such mortgages suited less well the needs of banks and near banks because their liabilities were much shorter term. A credit union, for example, exposed itself to considerable risk if it made a 25-year mortgage loan at a fixed 6.25 percent when it might later find itself required to pay in excess of 12 percent interest to attract deposits to finance the loan (as was the case in 1981 and 1982). After 1969, NHA regulations were changed, the terms of residential mortgages became much more flexible, and banks, credit unions and trust companies found residential mortgages more attractive while life companies found them less so. Trust and mortgage loan companies in particular grew very rapidly (see table 24) because their chief liability, a type of term deposit called guaranteed investment certificates (GICs), is well suited to mortgage lending. GICs are issued for periods of up to five years, which for a long time was the most popular mortgage term, thereby enabling trust and mortgage loan companies to match maturities of assets and liabilities.

As the shorter term of residential mortgages made them less attractive to life companies, they turned to non-residential mortgages with longer terms (see Hatch 1972, chapter 12). Unfortunately, we have data back to 1976 only, but these are sufficient to show the trend. At the end of 1976, 41.3 percent of life insurance companies mortgage assets were non-residential, and this increased to 56.2 percent by the end of 1986.

Stocks

The proportion of life companies financial assets held in the form of stocks (common and preferred shares) rose from 2.38 percent in 1961 to 8.35 percent in 1986, as shown in table 26. This growth also shows up when life companies share assets are considered as a proportion of the total value of stocks held by all sectors of the economy, which figure grew from 1.02 percent in 1961 to 3.21 percent in 1986 (see table 27). The chief reason for this increase lies in the rapid growth of life insurance policies and annuities (both individual and group pension plans) sold as variable contracts paying benefits which are not fixed in advance but which vary with the market value of a specified group of assets called segregated funds. These segregated funds have been the fastest growing component of the business, increasing from $2 million in 1961, the first year of regulatory permission, to $12,410 million in 1985. About 40 percent of all segregated fund assets in 1985 were in shares, while only about 5 percent of other life insurance assets were.

The growth of segregated funds may be related to the desire of policyholders and annuitants to hold contingent claims which will offer some protection against unforeseen inflation. More traditional policies suffered severely from rising inflation. A policy issued with a face value of $10,000 in 1961, with then current market interest rates factored into the calculation of its premiums and into the calculation of its cash value, was inadequate in terms of purchasing power in 1986, and it paid a dismal rate of return, *ex post*, on its savings portion (cash value). No wonder the call of the industry's critics to "buy term and invest the rest" instead of buying whole life was appealing to many.

PROPERTY/CASUALTY INSURANCE COMPANIES

Like other financial intermediaries, such as banks which issue deposits and invest in loans, property and casualty insurance companies issue contingent claims against accidental property loss and liability judgments and invest in bonds, stocks and short-term assets.

About 60 percent of the funds required to purchase the industry's assets are represented by liabilities to policyholders. There are small amounts of bank loans and deposits, but almost all the remainder of the same side of the balance sheet is equity. Liabilities to policyholders are recognized on the industry's balance sheet as resulting from the time lag between receipt of cash premiums and the payment of claims. Premiums are paid in advance for the most part, and claims are paid with a lag after being incurred by the insured event.

Equity funds are provided largely from retained earnings (as well as from new share issues and advances from parent corporations), and the amount of equity in turn determines the ability of firms to take on more insurance business. Hence, profits are a major source of the size and growth of assets.

The pre-tax profitability of the industry is highly variable, as shown in figure 3. The industry prefers to focus public attention on underwriting gain, which is the difference between premium income earned and net claims incurred for the period. If we examine data for the years 1968-85, the years for which industry data are reported in *Financial Institutions* (Statistics Canada catalogue 61-005), we see that underwriting gain was positive in only four out of 18 years. Investment income as a proportion of total assets was quite stable over the period, while underwriting gain as a fraction of total assets varied widely over time. As a result of the cyclical behaviour of the latter, profit (underwriting gain plus investment income) as a percentage of total assets or return on assets (ROA) was also highly cyclical, as was return on equity (ROE) which averaged 9.94 percent over the 1968-85 period. The average rate of investment income return on assets was 6.35 percent for the same period.

Like the Bank of Canada, property/casualty insurance companies are in the enviable position of not paying interest on their liabilities. Unlike the

Figure 3
Profit Ratios for Property/Casualty Insurance

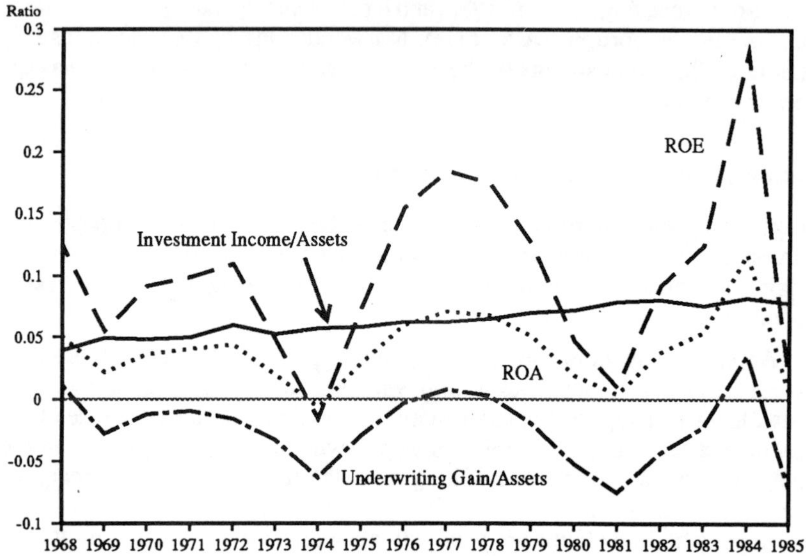

Bank, they are in the position that competition tends to drive their rate of return on equity to levels comparable with other industries. Competition forces premium rates down to a level resulting in losses on underwriting accounts. Underwriting return cannot be divorced from investment income. The two sources of income must be considered together, just as in the case of chartered banks where service charges must be considered together with investment income.

The asset side of the balance sheet of property and casualty insurance companies is shown in table 28. Short-term assets form a larger fraction of the portfolio than is the case for life companies, a fact which is consistent with our earlier observation on the desirability of matching the terms of assets and liabilities. Property/casualty companies' liabilities are shorter term than those of life companies. Bonds are favoured over mortgages because of the need for liquidity. The increase in mortgage investments after 1966 is also consistent with our earlier observations on the changing character of residential mortgages, a change toward shorter terms. Improvements in secondary market liquidity should improve the attractiveness of mortgages as investments.

The property and casualty insurance industry is so small in relation to the rest of the economy that it is not a major player in the market for any financial instrument, as is shown in table 29. Only in the bond market do we see

Table 28

Property and Casualty Insurance Companies' Asset Structure
(asset items as a percentage of total financial assets)

	1961	1966	1971	1976	1981	1986
Cash and Deposits	7.09	5.69	6.17	8.32	7.22	5.19
Treasury Bills	0.23	0.80	0.24	0.25	2.20	3.97
Short-Term Paper	0.08	1.35	1.41	3.70	4.01	3.28
Subtotal: Cash, TBs, S-T Paper	7.40	7.84	7.83	12.28	13.42	12.45
Mortgages	0.99	1.05	1.69	2.99	3.18	2.62
Bonds	64.99	61.01	58.04	54.87	50.27	49.95
Stocks	7.70	12.18	15.23	13.23	12.85	13.52
Foreign Investment	6.71	4.29	2.77	1.58	1.39	0.98
Other Assets	4.81	5.79	6.62	2.79	5.46	8.04
Total Assets	100.00	100.00	100.00	100.00	100.00	100.00

Source: National Balance Sheet Accounts.

Table 29

Assets of Property and Casualty Insurance Companies
As a Percentage of Total Held by All Sectors of the Economy

	1961	1966	1971	1976	1981	1986
Total Financial Assets	0.732	0.701	0.725	0.781	0.646	0.914
Treasury Bills	0.159	0.737	0.209	0.217	1.250	1.198
Short-Term Paper	0.167	2.090	1.324	2.671	2.109	1.353
Mortgages	0.113	0.102	0.152	0.246	0.258	0.271
Bonds	2.289	2.413	2.533	2.847	2.378	2.485
Stocks	0.450	0.622	1.031	1.103	0.883	1.023

Source: National Balance Sheet Accounts.

these companies holding as much as 2.8 percent of the value of bonds outstanding.

SUMMARY AND CONCLUSIONS

The size of life insurance company financial assets relative to total financial assets has been declining throughout the post World War II period. In particular, the industry's holdings of total mortgage assets has declined precipitously, in relative terms, since the 1960s when about 30 percent of all mortgages in Canada were held by the industry to about 13 percent in recent years. A change in NHA mortgages from 25- to 5-year term has been the chief cause of this change in the mortgage market.

Total financial assets of property/casualty companies have constituted less than 1 percent of the total financial assets of all sectors, with no strong trend over the past 25 years.

Government tax policy has had a profound effect on the demand for life insurance and on the product mix. Policies which have encouraged savings through tax-sheltered RRSPs have increased demand for annuities both by individuals who initially register their RRSPs with a life company and by those who purchase a life annuity upon maturity of an RRSP originally registered with another financial institution.

Tax rules permitting income averaging annuities during the 1970s caused a booming demand, followed by a collapse in 1981 when tax rules were changed.

Apart from shifts in product demand caused by tax changes, there has been a pronounced trend away from whole life policies and toward term insurance (individual and group). This has resulted in lower amounts of funds under the control of life companies and has been the single most important factor explaining the secular decline in the relative size of insurance company assets.

Direct regulation of the Canadian insurance industry (both life and property/casualty) has been aimed at protecting policyholders by ensuring solvency. Regulation of asset portfolios has been designed with this in mind, but in practice there is little evidence that portfolio regulation has been influential on the companies' decisions.

According to Hill (1986), insurance regulation in many countries has aimed at redirecting financial investment and thereby the flow of real resources. Some countries, such as India, have sought to encourage local government finance and also the housing sector. Most countries have sought to promote domestic investment and curtail investment abroad. Canada belongs with the majority and has required insurance companies to limit acquisition of foreign assets. Given the relatively small size of insurance company assets and the ability of households (the ultimate wealth holders) to make offsetting adjustments in their portfolios, it is doubtful that such regulation has much effect.

Chapter 6

Innovation and Information

INTRODUCTION

This chapter contains a selective survey of topics of intense current interest to economists and policymakers. The first section discusses product (marketing) innovation and process (production) innovation. The second section briefly surveys the relevant research on information asymmetries between buyers and sellers and search costs in the insurance market. The third section discusses an important recent case of innovation in market structure, namely the growth of captive insurance companies. The fourth section reports an economic viewpoint on the controversial subject of differentiation by age and sex in the setting of insurance rates.

Technological change over time is at least as important as gains in allocative efficiency which result from changing the scale and scope of operations within the technological limitations at a point in time (i.e., from exploitation of scale and scope economies). Innovation in production technology has a significant positive impact on the rate of technological change. However, in many circumstances there may be a trade-off between improvements in production efficiency through innovation and the loss of allocative efficiency through spillovers which allow firms to freely benefit from the innovations undertaken by rival firms (see Bernstein and Nadiri 1988).

Based on our output measure as reported in chapter 4, the life insurance industry's achievements in productivity improvement have been considerable. Property/casualty has done less well, probably because of a string of relatively unprofitable years. The insurance industry's productivity improvements may still be less than what could be achieved.

PRODUCT INNOVATION

The industry is not considered to be particularly innovative in designing new products nor in attracting new customers. The life insurance industry has appeared to be reactive rather than innovative. Universal life, a product popular in the 1980s, was invented in the U.S. but only well after years of criticism in both countries of the industry's chief product, whole life. Chapter 5 has traced the relative decline in the industry which resulted from the fading popularity of whole life. Many would argue that the industry was slow to introduce new and better products. The growth of the industry during the 1970s was attributable in part to government policy on RRSPs, not to industry innovation. The industry has, for the most part, resisted the trend to term insurance and has resisted innovations in marketing. For example, the A.R. Williams agency has been successful in selling life insurance through a network of part-time agents in the U.S., but it has been resisted in its efforts to penetrate the Canadian market. Such a system offers the possibility of distributional efficiencies and most economists would want the market, not regulators, to decide whether it should survive.

When different life insurance premium rates for smokers and non-smokers were introduced about ten years ago, the industry's bias again became apparent as some firms complained that the innovators would skim the cream of the market by attracting low risk non-smokers and leaving the other companies with a pool of high risk individuals—an "unfair" result given that the older policies' premium rates were based on risks for smokers and non-smokers averaged together. In any event, most companies eventually introduced non-smokers' policies without harming the industry. This example illustrates a more general issue. The industry has always opposed sales efforts designed to convince the consumer to drop one policy and buy another (industry opposition is enshrined in "anti-twisting" laws which forbid this). This strikes most observers as anti-competitive and inimical to consumers' interests.

One can understand the industry's position in the light of its cost and commission structure. Commissions and other costs are usually higher than premiums in the first year of a policy. Agents have an incentive to sell a new replacement policy—especially to the customer of another firm—but the firms have an incentive to prevent policy lapses and switches. As a result of this incentive structure, firms oppose the freer competition which is in the consumer's interest.

If we turn away from product innovation to consideration of process innovation, which refers to the application of new and improved techniques of production, we find few studies explaining the causes of productivity change. Notable exceptions are the contributions of Globerman (1984, 1986) who studied factors determining the adoption of electronic data processing (EDP) equipment in the insurance industry. In an empirical analysis of the relationship between insurer size and EDP innovation, he found evidence "that large insurers in the U.S. and Canada were, if anything, slower to computerize their head office activities than their smaller rivals. This observation is consistent with [Globerman's] finding that the productivity impacts of automation decrease as one includes the largest insurers in the sample. The findings suggest caution in taking a benign attitude toward large mergers in the financial sector" (Globerman 1986:292). Some large mergers could have consequences on innovation that outweigh any potential allocative efficiency gains.

INFORMATION ASYMMETRIES

In recent years a number of economists have developed the hypothesis of information asymmetries in the marketplace. Sellers and buyers are postulated to hold different information as regards, for example, the quality or characteristics of the good to be sold or purchased. These asymmetries, it is argued, persist because of differential costs in acquiring information and are important because of differences in incentives for the two sides of the market. While these concepts have excited the interest of many researchers, others are doubtful of their empirical significance.

Two important types of information asymmetry are distinguished in insurance markets. Adverse selection results from information asymmetry in favour of the buyer who has information about his true risk class (e.g., his state of health or the care with which he drives) which is not available to the seller. The buyer's incentive is to represent himself as a low risk in order to qualify for a low premium rate. Sellers are not able to costlessly ascertain the truth. The phrase adverse selection refers to the case where a seller offers a single premium rate to a heterogeneous group and those buyers who know themselves to be risky find the offer more attractive. High risk individuals are adversely selected as customers. Such information asymmetry favours consumers against firms but in the extreme may prevent an insurance market from existing (see Rothschild and Stiglitz 1976 for a seminal paper).

The reverse asymmetry favours firms against individuals who lack knowledge of the price and quality characteristics of the product. Mathewson (1983) develops a model characterized by variation in marginal search costs for rational but not fully informed consumers. Price discrimination across consumers by firms is possible as each individual contract sale is a negotiated bilateral exchange between a consumer and life insurance agent who knows how consumers respond to price changes through information revealed by potential consumers. The asymmetric information which favours the agent enables him to sell essentially similar products at different prices to different consumers.

Dahlby and West (1986) test a model of costly consumer search using automobile insurance data for Alberta for the period 1974-81. They select compulsory third-party liability insurance as a homogeneous product, rates for which vary by age, sex, marital status and geographic location of the driver. They argue that their empirical results support costly consumer search as an explanation for price variability across sellers, a conclusion similar to Mathewson's.

CAPTIVE INSURANCE COMPANIES

Captive insurance companies sell insurance only to the customer or customers who have established them and who own them. They often operate offshore for tax reasons. The growth of captive insurance companies and offshore re-insurance has been an important phenomenon in both Canada and the U.S. Since little has been written on the subject in Canada, we refer to a U.S. study (Davey 1979) which focuses on taxation as the driving force for growth of captives. As such, this affords an example of the significance of tax considerations in the growth of domestic versus foreign production.

The U.S. tax code prevents corporations from deducting contributions to reserves for the purpose of self-insurance, so firms must buy insurance from property/casualty companies or set up a captive insurance company to serve them. By paying premiums to a captive company, the parent benefits by retaining control over reserves and perhaps by reducing transactions costs. He may also benefit by reducing moral hazard (the parent has no incentive to engage in behaviour which would increase the risk of the insured event, whereas he might if fully insured with an independent insurer), or he may benefit by exiting from a pool of other insurees who are on average more risky than himself (where information asymmetry prevents him from communicating a credible signal of this fact and receiving a more favourable rate). A captive insurance company may serve one of a group of companies or hospitals or government agencies and may be created to serve an unmet need for insurance. The captive is often an offshore company, little more than a shell, which acts as a re-insurer for the insurance business of a traditional property/casualty company that "fronts" for the captive and handles premium collections and claims adjustment in return for a share of the gross premium paid by the parent corporation. Gross premiums less the front's costs are paid entirely as re-insurance premiums to the captive who holds reserves from which the claims vetted by the front are paid.

The U.S. Internal Revenue Service soon ruled that in the case of a one-to-one relationship between parent and captive, this was no more than a means of bypassing regulations against deducting contributions to self-insurance reserves. This ruling was followed by moves by captives to acquire third-party re-insurance business. The point of recounting these events is to illustrate the significance of tax legislation on the growth of the industry where, in this case, legislation caused growth of offshore activity.

Canada's experience with offshore (but not captive) re-insurance companies has been tainted in some instances by allegations of fraud. Domestic insurance companies could (for a while, until the regulators clamped down on the use of unregistered re-insurance companies) re-insure heavily with offshore companies and thereby do a large volume of business with very little capitalization. Some of this insurance business might be very risky. Perhaps some was sold below competitive rates. The re-insurance company relied on the Canadian seller to properly screen buyers and assign them to their correct risk class. Because much of the risk was passed on to the re-insurer, the incentive to screen accurately was attenuated. Unregistered insurers also lacked full incentive to monitor the quality of this business because they could, in the event of serious trouble, renege by claiming faulty screening by the Canadian company or declare bankruptcy and remain outside the reach of Canadian authorities.

DIFFERENTIALS BY AGE AND SEX IN INSURANCE RATES

Life insurance and annuity rates have always discriminated on the basis of life expectancy. Since it is infeasible to obtain necessary information to estimate the probability distribution of life expectancy on an individual basis, differentiation is made on the basis of information which is inexpensive to obtain: age, sex, smoking habits and a few readily obtained indicators of individual and ancestors' health status. Similarly, automobile insurance rates are partly based on age, sex, marital status and geographical region.

In recent years a movement has begun to remove premium differentials based on categorical discrimination among age and sex groups. Differential pension contributions or benefits based on sex have been challenged and, in some cases, removed. Differential auto insurance rates based on driver age have been challenged and, in some cases, removed (e.g., in B.C.).

Some would object to categorical discrimination on the grounds of equity. Women currently pay more for the same benefit or receive less in benefits for the same contribution because they tend to live longer. If women are seen as deserving a wealth transfer, then "uni-sex" rates make sense. But the equity argument is not consistent, since women would lose from "uni-sex" life insurance rates which are currently lower for women because of their greater longevity. Crocker and Snow (1986) argue that whatever the equity grounds for such anti-discrimination policies, they are obtained at some cost inefficiency, although they are unable to quantify the efficiency loss. Moore

(1987) argues that uni-sex pension plans significantly raise the costs to employers of female labour and will result in reduced wages or increased unemployment among women. Since women, on average, live longer than men, women's pension benefits exceed men's. If women's contributions are equalized with men's, the employer must pay the difference. The employer will then either avoid hiring women or seek to recover the higher pension costs by paying lower wages to women.

SUMMARY AND CONCLUSIONS

The life insurance industry has been reactive rather than innovative in designing and promoting new products. This conservative stance has contributed to the decline of the industry relative to other financial institutions—at least as measured by assets. However, as measured by contribution to GDP in constant dollars, the industry has grown at above average rates (see chapter 2). The pace of product innovation appears to have increased since the latter part of the last decade, and the industry's prospects for the future appear to be strong on this score.

While direct evidence on particular process innovations is scarce, the overall evidence of productivity growth (shown in chapter 4) reflects very favourably on the life insurance industry but less favourably on the property/liability insurance industry. Globerman's studies of the introduction of computers in the insurance industry found some evidence that larger firms were less innovative than smaller firms.

The growth of captive insurance companies and offshore re-insurance has been one of the most important innovations in the structure of the property/casualty insurance industry in recent years in both Canada and the U.S. To a large extent, this growth appears to have been driven by tax considerations, at least in the U.S.

The theories of information asymmetry (as between buyers and sellers) and of the costly acquisition of information have been applied to the insurance industry. These theories are enlisted to explain price dispersion and price discrimination in insurance markets. However, one could as well explain price dispersion in terms of as yet unmeasured variations across sellers in product quality and product characteristics, and we must conclude that there is not yet a generally agreed explanation of price dispersion.

In recent years there has been a movement to remove differentials in auto insurance premiums based on age and sex and to remove differentials in pension (annuity) contributions based on sex. This movement has been based on a search for equity but it is likely to have unintended effects in terms of both equity and efficiency. For example, uni-sex pension plans may raise employers' costs of female labour, resulting in reduced wages or reduced employment for women.

Chapter 7

Industrial Development, Policy Issues and Conclusions

INTRODUCTION

Government is concerned with the efficient functioning of the insurance industry. It is also concerned with the equitable treatment of producers and consumers in the marketplace. The government employs a number of instruments to control the insurance industry, the most significant policy levers being regulation and competition and tax policies.

In order to formulate appropriate policies, government needs information on growth, employment, productivity and prices in insurance services, as well as information on the effects of regulation and taxation policy and the inadvertent impacts of policies in areas other than insurance. In this chapter each of these topics is discussed, pulling together the relevant evidence developed in other chapters. We recognize that in many areas of concern to policymakers there is insufficient evidence to support a consensus among economists. However, policy decisions cannot be delayed in the face of constant cries for more research. In this chapter, we suppress scholarly caution and draw conclusions as best we can.

PRODUCTION AND DEMAND

Over the period 1961-85, the insurance industry (life and property/casualty combined) has grown in real terms at the same rate as all industries combined—4.4 percent per year compounded—which is considerably faster than manufacturing at 4.1 percent per year but slower than total services at 4.7 percent. The two insurance industry components have grown at widely disparate rates—2.8 percent annual growth for property/casualty but 5.8 percent for life insurance.

The analysis of the effects of income growth on consumers in chapter 3 helps explain the growth of insurance services. Over the period 1952 to 1983, we estimated an income elasticity of demand for insurance services (life and property/casualty combined) of about 1.5. For non-insurance services the estimated income elasticity is about 1.25; for non-durables and semi-durables it is less than 1.0. These results imply a secular trend which is higher than the growth rate of income, assuming relative prices are constant. Our analysis also reveals a high price elasticity of demand for insurance services, which implies a strong negative impact on demand and on industry sales revenue from price increases. Property/casualty insurance prices grew faster than the total consumer price index (CPI) during 1971 to 1985, but the price of life insurance services, by our measure, grew at a slower rate. This difference in price performance helps to explain the difference in growth of demand.

The prices of goods other than insurance also influence insurance demand. When the prices of other goods rise, demand for insurance rises. The effect is particularly strong for durable goods. As their prices rise, more insurance is demanded to cover their increased value.

In addition to income and price effects, consumer demand is significantly influenced by other (demographic) characteristics of households. Demand for property insurance rises with age of household head but falls for life insurance. The aging of Canada's population has obvious implications for future demand when combined with this result. The reverse pattern holds for size of household: demand falls with size of household for property insurance but rises for life insurance. If the decline in average household size in Canada continues, it has implications for future demand. We find that female household heads spend more on property insurance and less on life insurance than otherwise similarly situated male household heads. Tenant households spend much less on property insurance than do homeowners. Demand for both types of insurance is significantly higher in Quebec than in other provinces.

EMPLOYMENT AND PRODUCTIVITY

Insurance industry employment constituted about 1 percent of total employment in 1985 and has grown at about 1.3 percent per year over 1961-85, slower than total employment. The positive effect on employment of the rapid growth of life insurance output was partly offset by the rapid growth of productivity in this industry component.

The quality of insurance jobs, as evidenced by average weekly earnings, is higher than in all industries combined and higher than in other finance, insurance and real estate industries. The common prejudice against service sector jobs as being inferior to manufacturing is contradicted in the case of insurance.

There has long been a concern about the apparent discrepancy between productivity growth in the services sector and the manufacturing sector. The shift in employment and production in favour of services appears to foretell a slowdown in productivity performance in the economy and a consequent slowdown in the rate of improvement in living standards. By and large, the official statistics support the opinion that productivity improvement is slower in services.

The story told by the official statistics is probably biased. The quality and validity of the output measures for service industries are inferior to those for manufacturing industries. For some service industries, output is proxied by labour input, resulting in zero labour productivity growth by definition. Some would argue that this is the result of the difficulty of defining and measuring service output, but we would argue it is the result of decades of relative neglect. Research and development of service output measures has been underfunded as has basic survey work. In support of our view we offer our results for the life insurance industry which show labour productivity growth of 3.95 percent per year during 1961-85, which compares to 3.08 percent in manufacturing for the same period.

Our analysis in chapter 4 also contains estimates of total factor productivity for life and property/casualty combined, revealing a respectable growth of about 1 percent per year compounded over 1977 to 1984.

FOREIGN TRADE

The bulk of insurance exports are earned on insured exported merchandise and vice versa for imports. Thus, trade in merchandise drives trade in services. Both exports and imports are in the range of 5 to 7 percent of the total value of insurance services produced in Canada, with exports equal to about 80 to 90 percent of imports. The re-insurance market is international in scope, and companies in Canada (especially property/casualty companies) purchase significant amounts of re-insurance services abroad.

Canadian life companies, in their global operations, earned about $5.6 billion or 40 percent of their premium income abroad in 1985, but this international success is little reflected in the balance of payments figures because these premiums are earned by foreign subsidiaries of Canadian companies and as such are treated as transactions between non-resident corporations and non-resident institutions, not as cross-border transactions. Only the net revenues of Canadian insurance companies from operations abroad are recorded in the balance of payments.

Canada, along with most foreign countries, requires that domestic assets be held by all companies against domestic liabilities. This type of regulation is a form of protectionism which reduces international trade in insurance services.

One benefit of international competition is to improve the efficiency of domestic suppliers. This has been achieved as evidenced by the fact that Canadian life insurance firms have been highly successful in their foreign operations. In 1985, over 40 percent of Canadian federally registered companies' global business was outside Canada.

COMPETITION POLICY AND MERGERS

The degree of competition and the incentive to merge in the insurance industry is determined in part by the extent to which economies of scale (specialization) and economies of scope (diversity) exist. A production process is said to display economies of scale if cost increases by less than a given proportional increase in all outputs produced. Diseconomies of scale refer to the converse case.

The question of economies of scale is relevant to the issue of horizontal merger policy. Mergers in the presence of economies of scale can reduce unit costs of production and thereby increase efficiency within the industry. On the other hand, mergers within an industry when scale economies do not exist may just lead to increased monopolization and the inefficiency which results from price in excess of marginal cost. The evidence on economies of scale in the life insurance industry as cited in chapter 4 is neutral, for the most part. Economies of scale are not large for firms producing 5 percent, or even less, of industry output and neither is there strong evidence of diseconomies of scale for the largest firms. Mergers will neither significantly reduce competition nor improve the efficiency with which industry output is produced.

The data on industry concentration reported in table 30 provide little cause for concern. The percentage of the market controlled by the four largest property/casualty firms has risen over the 1961-85 period but remains very low at 9.2 percent in 1961 and 18.1 percent in 1985. On the other hand, the control by the four largest life companies is much greater at over 40 percent; but the trend is down.

A policy of easy entry for both Canadian and foreign companies has helped to prevent undue concentration, and such policies should be continued.

The concept of economies of scope is an important extension to the older concept of economies of scale. This new concept recognizes the multiproduct nature of most firms. In life insurance, economies of scope may result from the cost savings associated with the sales efforts of an agent who

Table 30
Four Firm Concentration Ratios

Property/Casualty Insurance
in-Canada business of federally registered companies, excluding Lloyds and all accident and sickness business
(net premiums written)

	1961	1971	1981	1985
4 largest (%)	9.2	11.9	15.6	18.1

Life Insurance
federally registered companies
(life insurance assets, excluding accident and sickness)

	1961	1971	1981	1985
4 largest (%)	46.4	44.2	40.6	42.7

can provide a variety of term, whole life and annuity policies. Economies of scope may result from joint production of property/liability and life insurance products, or from joint production of insurance, deposit, loan and security sales services. The existence of economies of scope plays an important role in the determination of the efficiency consequences of conglomerate mergers. These mergers are relevant to entry deregulation of the four pillars: insurance, banks, security dealers, and trust companies. Eliminating barriers to entry would permit the sort of "one-stop financial shopping" pioneered by Sears, American Express and others in the U.S. The existence of significant economies of scope is the key to the efficiency gains of such production. Yet evidence is scarce or non-existent. As stated in chapter 4, there is only one study on economies of scope in the insurance industry that we know of, and the results are for life insurance products only. It was found that economies of scope are rather weak. No one has investigated for economies of scope among life insurance and property/liability insurance products.

REGULATION

Federal regulation of the life insurance industry has historically been prudential, aimed at ensuring the financial health of the industry and safety for policyholders by requiring that policy reserves meet certain standards and that investments be conservative and low risk. A mortgage cannot be issued for more than 75 percent of a property's value. A limited fraction (now 25 percent) of a life company's portfolio can be invested in equity issues, and these must meet certain standards in terms of their history of cash dividends. A limited fraction (10 percent) of a portfolio can be in the form of real property. Life companies are required to hold Canadian assets in proportion to their Canadian business.

Federal regulations require property and casualty companies to maintain assets (valued at market prices) in excess of liabilities by a margin of at least 15 percent.

Entry has been relatively free into both industries but each life company has, until 1987, been limited in the maximum percentage it can hold of the common stock of any one company (30 percent, with some exceptions such as realty companies). Deregulation of financial markets, beginning in 1987, removes most ownership barriers. The precise details of new legislation were still the subject of debate at the time this study was written, which fact limits our ability to comment on the effects of deregulation.

In addition to regulating the affairs of provincially licensed companies, the provinces regulate the licensing of agents. The restriction of sales channels for life insurance, in particular, is an important issue. Many would argue that inefficient distribution is a prime policy concern. Deregulation offered the opportunity to improve insurance retailing by, for example, permitting life companies to sell through subsidiary trust companies, which they are allowed to own as of 1987. This particular retailing possibility is now in doubt as it has been actively opposed by life insurance agents who feel that the public requires service from an expert and specialized sales staff.

Only firms licensed by the federal or provincial governments to sell life insurance in Canada may do so. This restriction could have proven to be highly protectionist but for the fact that Canadian regulations have always permitted foreign firms to become licensed and to operate in Canada. This contrasts with the heavy restrictions placed on foreign banks in Canada prior to the 1980 Bank Act revisions.

TAXATION

In chapter 5 we analysed the impact of tax-sheltered individual savings vehicles (RRSPs) on the growth of the life insurance industry. We also note here that the industry shares in the growth of another tax-sheltered savings vehicle, namely trusteed pension plans for groups of employees, with life companies controlling a minority share of the assets.

Since 1969, life companies have been taxed on both their business profits and their investment income. The industry is particularly sensitive to taxation of investment income as such taxes fall more heavily on whole life rather than term insurance, thereby inhibiting the growth of their most profitable product. Whole life has a savings component, unlike pure (term) insurance, and the associated reserves and investment income are larger for whole life.

We have argued at several points in this study that the prepayment of property and casualty insurance premiums and the lag in payment of claims results in an interest free loan by policyholders to companies. Companies use these loans to acquire interest earning assets, and they pay taxes on the resulting investment income. We have also argued that competition forces premium rates to reflect the interest opportunity cost on these loans. Thus, consumers pay lower premiums than they would if explicit cash interest were paid on these loans. As things now stand, consumers barter the use of money for reduced premiums and, as with other barter transactions, the Canadian System of National Accounts should reflect this via imputed interest income and an equal imputed increase in consumer expenditure on premiums. For insurance purchased by the business sector as intermediate inputs, the increased imputed interest income exactly balances the increased imputed premium expense and there is no net increase in GDP. For insurance purchased by the personal sector, investment income and personal expenditure rise equally and therefore so does GDP.

The point in repeating this analysis here is that our argument would appear to justify taxation of imputed interest income to individuals. Since imputed interest is not currently taxed in the hands of individuals, the industry benefits. Business sector (purchaser) imputed income is offset by business sector imputed expense, so taxable profits would be unchanged. Similarly, property/casualty companies' imputed revenue and expense would be equal with no change in their taxable income. The federal government in 1986/87 has, in fact, considered related questions of taxation of imputed interest on deposits.

Some of the most significant effects of government policy on the industry have been inadvertent results of changes in tax legislation and in government programmes which were designed with other goals in mind. The effects on the insurance industry were major but incidental to the original purpose. For example, the major purpose of introducing individual tax-sheltered savings plans (RRSPs) was to assist individuals in providing for their retirement years. But as shown in chapter 5, RRSPs had a major impact on the growth of the life insurance industry. Other examples—the enhancement of death, disability, dependent survivor and retirement benefits under the Canada and Quebec Pension Plans—have had an effect on the demand for privately supplied substitutes for these products.

Assets indexed to inflation are not offered by the private sector in Canada, but they have been available in the form of indexed pensions to federal government employees. In the U.K., inflation indexed bonds have been available to retired individuals ("granny bonds"). There is clearly a demand in Canada for such instruments as seen by the demand for indexed pensions. International experience has shown that, with few exceptions, only governments offer such instruments. These bonds, if issued by the Canadian government, could be bought by private sector financial intermediaries, including life companies, as backing for RRSPs, resulting in increased demand for annuities.

CONCLUSIONS

Two sets of factors are driving insurance industry output and employment growth. First, a high responsiveness of consumer demand and industry revenue to income growth and to price changes has favoured the life insurance industry. The price of life insurance services has risen by less than the inflation rate, while the reverse holds true for property/casualty. The influences of low income elasticity and high price inflation hamper the growth of the property/casualty industry. Secondly, industry growth, especially for life insurance, is strongly buffeted up and down by tax policy (RRSPs have had particular impact).

Industry productivity performance (especially for life insurance and less so for property/casualty) has been healthy. The speed of product innovation has been improving in the last decade and will receive fresh impetus from deregulation.

Government regulation has focused on ensuring prudential management of assets to guard against default to policyholders. The life insurance industry in particular has an enviable record in this regard, but it is unlikely that government regulation is the major cause of this success. The industry itself is very conscious of the necessity for preserving a good reputation.

The competitive health of the industry is evidenced by low concentration ratios, easy entry and lack of evidence of significant returns to scale. For the most part, merger policy can be contented with benign neglect.

Tax policy has powerful effects on the industry and these effects are sometimes unforeseen, requiring care in the formulation of tax initiatives.

Deregulation will soon have significant and largely unforeseeable effects on the industry, but one opportunity for efficiency improvement may already be slipping away. Distribution channels for life insurance are likely to remain monopolized by life companies instead of being made more competitive by allowing trust companies and banks to sell the product. It may be true, as the insurance industry argues, that policyholders are best served by specialized agents, but it would be better to let the market decide how specialized these agents must be and not leave the decision to regulatory edict.

The analysis of the insurance industry, like all service industries, is in its infancy. Numerous important issues have been highlighted in this study which bear on effective policy formulation and for which there is little or no empirical evidence. First, the issue of economies of product diversity or scope has to be investigated for both life and property/casualty insurance. Policies regarding the efficiency gains and losses of conglomerate mergers and deregulating financial services can only be answered with a knowledge of the extent of scope economies.

Secondly, changes in the regulatory and tax environments facing insurance companies will cause these firms to change the quantity and variety of their products and to alter their pricing strategy. Policymakers need to know how insurance firms will adjust. Coupled with this adjustment, there will be changes in employment and productivity brought about by any new policies.

The third issue pertains to the demand for insurance services. There is no evidence, apart from the analysis in chapter 3, on the determinants of demand for various types of insurance services, and on the characteristics of the consumers who contribute to determining demand for these services. Both the efficiency and equity implications of government regulatory and tax policies can only be evaluated when consideration is given to the effects on consumer welfare.

References

Allen, R.F., "Cross-Sectional Estimates of Cost Economies in Stock Property-Liability Companies," *Review of Economics and Statistics,* 56:1 (February 1974), pp. 100-103.

Baker, A.M., "Liberalization of Trade in Services—The World Insurance Industry," in O. Giarini, ed., *The Emerging Service Economy,* New York, Pergamon, 1987.

Belth, J.M., *The Retail Price Structure in American Life Insurance,* Bloomington, Indiana, Bureau of Business Research, Graduate School of Business, Indiana University, 1966.

Belth, J.M., "Author's Reply," *Journal of Risk and Insurance,* 36:4 (September 1969), pp. 495-496.

Benston, G.J., "Economies of Scale in Financial Institutions," *Journal of Money, Credit and Banking,* 4:2 (May 1972), pp. 312-341.

Bernstein, J.I., and M.I. Nadiri, "Research and Development, and Intraindustry Spillovers: An Empirical Application of Dynamic Duality," *Review of Economic Studies,* forthcoming 1988.

Blair, R.D., J.R. Jackson and R.J. Vogel, "Economies of Scale in the Administration of Health Insurance," *Review of Economics and Statistics,* 57:2 (May 1975), pp. 185-189.

Canadian Life and Health Insurance Facts, Toronto, Canadian Life and Health Insurance Association, annual. (Also referred to as CLHIA *Facts.*)

Colenutt, D.W., "Economies of Scale in the United Kingdom Ordinary Life Assurance Industry," *Applied Economics,* 9:3 (September 1977), pp. 219-225.

Crocker, K.J. and A. Snow, "The Efficiency Effects of Categorical Discrimination in the Insurance Industry," *Journal of Political Economy,* 44:2 (April 1986), pp. 321-44.

Cummins, J.D., "Economics of Scale in Independent Insurance Agencies," *Journal of Risk and Insurance,* 44:4 (December 1977), pp. 539-553.

Cummins, J.D., H.S. Denenberg and W.C. Scheel, "Concentration in the U.S. Life Insurance Industry," *Journal of Risk and Insurance,* 39:2 (June 1972), pp. 177-199.

Dahlby, B. and D.S. West, "Price Dispersion in an Automobile Insurance Market," *Journal of Political Economy,* 94:2 (1986), pp. 418-38.

Daly, M.J., P.S. Rao and R.R. Geehan, "Productivity, Scale Economies and Technical Progress in the Canadian Life Insurance Industry," *International Journal of Industrial Organization*, 3 (1985), pp. 345-361.

Daula, T.V., "Economies of Scale in the Life Insurance Industry: An Econometric Analysis," unpublished M.S. thesis, M.I.T., 1976.

Davey, P.J., *Managing Risks Through Captive Insurance Companies*, New York, The Conference Board, Inc., 1979.

Deaton, A. and J. Muellbauer, *Economics and Consumer Behavior*, London, Cambridge University Press, 1983.

Deaton, A. and J. Muellbauer, "An Almost Ideal Demand System," *American Economic Review*, 70 (1980), pp. 312-336.

Denny, M., "Measuring the Real Output of the Life Insurance Industry: A Comment," *Review of Economics and Statistics*, 62:1 (February 1980), pp. 150-152.

Ehrlich, I. and G. Becker, "Market Insurance, Self Insurance and Self Protection," *Journal of Political Economy*, 80 (1972), pp. 623-648.

Geehan, R., "Returns to Scale in the Life Insurance Industry," *Bell Journal of Economics*, 8:2 (Autumn 1977), pp. 497-514.

Globerman, S., *The Adoption of Computer Technology by Insurance Companies*, Ottawa, Supply and Services Canada, 1984.

Globerman, S., "Firm Size and Dynamic Efficiency in the Life Insurance Industry," *Journal of Risk and Insurance*, June 1986, pp. 278-93.

Gold, B., "Changing Perspectives on Size, Scale, and Returns: An Interpretative Survey," *Journal of Economic Literature*, 19:1 (March 1981), pp. 5-33.

Halpern, P.J. and G.F. Mathewson, "Economies of Scale in Financial Institutions: A General Model Applied to Insurance," *Journal of Monetary Economics*, 1:2 (April 1975), pp. 203-220.

Hammond, J.D., E.R. Melander and M. Shilling, "Economies of Scale in the Property and Liability Insurance Industry," *Journal of Risk and Insurance*, 38:2 (June 1971), pp. 181-191.

Hatch, J.E., *The Canadian Mortgage Market*, Toronto, Queen's Printer for Ontario, 1975.

Hensley, Roy J., "Economies of Scale in Financial Enterprises," *Journal of Political Economy*, 66:5 (October 1958), pp. 389-398.

Hill, R.D., "Profit Regulation in Property-Liability Insurance," *Bell Journal of Economics*, 10:1 (Spring 1979), pp. 172-191.

Hill, R.D., "Insurance and Financial Intermediation," in *The Insurance Industry in Economic Development*, B. Wasow and R.D. Hill, eds., New York, NYU Press, 1986.

Hirshhorn, R. and R. Geehan, "Measuring the Real Output of the Life Insurance Industry," *Review of Economics and Statistics*, 49:2 (May 1977), pp. 211-219.

Houston, D.B. and R.M. Simon, "Economies of Scale in Financial Institutions: A Study in Life Insurance," *Econometrica*, 38:6 (November 1970), pp. 856-864.

Johnston, J. and G.W. Murphey, "The Growth of Life Assurance in the U.S. Since 1880," *Manchester School of Economics and Social Sciences*, 25:2 (May 1957), pp. 107-182.

Jorgenson, D. W., L.J. Lau and T.M. Stoker, "The Transcendental Logarithmic Model of Aggregate Consumer Behaviour," in *Advances in Econometrics*, vol. I, New York, JAI Press, 1982.

Joskow, P.L., "Cartels, Competition and Regulation in the Property-Liability Insurance Industry," *Bell Journal of Economics and Management Science*, 4:2 (Autumn 1973), pp. 375-427.

Kamerschen, D.R. and J.J. Pascucci, "The Retail Price Structure in American Life Insurance: Comment," *Journal of Risk and Insurance*, 36:4 (September 1969), pp. 493-495.

Kellner, S. and G.F. Mathewson, "Entry, Size Distribution, Scale, and Scope Economies in the Life Insurance Industry," *Journal of Business*, 56 (1983), pp. 25-44.

Mathewson, G.F., "Information, Search and Price Variability of Individual Life Insurance Contracts," *Journal of Industrial Economics*, 32:2 (December 1983), pp. 131-48.

May, J.D., and M. Denny, "Post-War Productivity in Canadian Manufacturing," *Canadian Journal of Economics*, 12 (1979), pp. 29-41.

Moore, R.L., "Are Male/Female Earnings Differentials Related to Life-Expectancy-Caused Pension Cost Differences?", *Economic Inquiry*, 35:3 (July 1987), pp. 389-401.

Neave, E.H., *Canada's Financial System*, Toronto, Wiley, 1981.

Neufeld, E.P., *The Financial System of Canada*, Toronto, Macmillan, 1982.

Pedoe, A., "The Trend of Life Insurance Company Expenses," *Transactions of the Society of Actuaries*, 4 (1952), pp. 482-510.

Pedoe, A., "Further Notes on the Trend of Life Insurance Company Expenses," *Transactions of the Society of Actuaries*, 13 (1961), pp. 1-30.

Phlips, L., *Applied Consumption Analysis*, New York, North Holland Publishing Co., 1983.

Praetz, P., "Returns to Scale in the U.S. Life Insurance Industry," *Journal of Risk and Insurance*, 47:3 (September 1980), pp. 525-533.

Praetz, P., "Returns to Scale in the Australian Life Insurance Industry," *Economic Record*, 55:158 (September 1981), pp. 269-275.

Pritchett, S.T., "An Intercompany Expense Comparison for 30 Life Insurers," *Journal of Risk and Insurance*, 38:4 (December 1971), pp. 552-562.

Pritchett, S.T., "Operating Expenses of Life Insurers, 1961-1970: Implications for Economies of Size," *Journal of Risk and Insurance*, 40:2 (June 1973), pp. 157-165.

Pritchett, S.T., "Operating Expenses and Prices for Thirty Insurers: Economies of Size for Ordinary Life Insurance," *Nebraska Journal of Economics and Business*, 13:2 (Spring 1974), pp. 19-31.

Pritchett, S.T. and J.E. Logan, "Economies of Size for Worker's Compensation Business," *Journal of Risk and Insurance*, 43:3 (September 1976), pp. 433-540.

Report of the Superintendent of Insurance for Canada, Volume 1, 1980, Ottawa, Supply and Services Canada, 1981.

Richards, K. and D. Colenutt, "Concentration in the U.K. Ordinary Life Assurance Market," *Journal of Industrial Economics*, 24:2 (December 1975), pp. 147-159.

Rothschild, M. and J. Stiglitz, "Equilibrium in Competitive Insurance Markets: An Essay on the Economics of Imperfect Information," *Quarterly Journal of Economics*, 90:2 (1976), pp. 629-55.

Rutledge, D.J.S. and R.H. Tuckwell, "Economies of Scale in Australian Life Insurance: An Empirical Note," *Economic Record*, 50:131 (September 1974), pp. 443-447.

Statistics Canada, *Financial Institutions*, catalogue 61-006, Ottawa, Supply and Services Canada, 1981.

Wasow, B., "Determinants of Insurance Penetration: A Cross-country Analysis," in B. Wasow and R.D. Hill, eds., *The Insurance Industry in Economic Development*, New York, NYU Press, 1986.

Weiss, Mary A., "Analysis of Productivity at the Firm Level: An Application to Life Insurers," *Journal of Risk and Insurance*, 53 (1986), pp. 49-84.

Winter, R.A., "On the Rate Structure of the American Life Insurance Market," *Journal of Finance*, 36:1 (March 1981), pp. 81-96.

